James Martin
Psychopolitics of Speech

Political Science | Volume 40

For Luis

James Martin is Professor of Political Theory at Goldsmiths, University of London. His research includes studies on Continental political theory, psychoanalysis, and rhetoric.

James Martin

Psychopolitics of Speech

Uncivil Discourse and the Excess of Desire

[transcript]

Bibliographic information published by the Deutsche Nationalbibliothek
The Deutsche Nationalbibliothek lists this publication in the Deutsche Nationalbibliografie; detailed bibliographic data are available in the Internet at http://dnb.d-nb.de

Cover layout: Maria Arndt, Bielefeld
Typeset by Michael Rauscher, Bielefeld
Printed by docupoint GmbH, Magdeburg
Print-ISBN 978-3-8376-3919-3
PDF-ISBN 978-3-8394-3919-7
https://doi.org/10.14361/9783839439197

Content

Preface 7

Introduction 9

1. Bodies of Speech 25

2. Voicing Desire 53

3. Talking to Excess 83

4. The Force of the Bitter Argument 109

5. An Ethics of Speech? 139

Conclusion 169

Bibliography 175

For Luis

Preface

This book originates in work undertaken for a Leverhulme Trust Research Fellowship from 2013–15 on 'Affective Rhetorical Strategies in Political Rhetoric'. I am grateful to the Trust for their support in that project, which produced various papers and a journal publication (see Martin, 2016), and to the organisers of various events at which some early ideas were developed as paper presentations. Versions of the text were delivered at: the University of Bath (2015); the Political Studies Association (PSA) conference in Sheffield (2015); the University of Essex (2016); the University of Bournemouth (2017); the Rhetoric Society of Europe Conference at the University of East Anglia (2017); Goldsmiths (2017); Oxford Brookes University (2018); and the PSA conference in Cardiff (2018). My gratitude also goes to the following for reading (or hearing) parts of the text and offering helpful insights and suggestions: Jakob Horstman at transcript; Jeremy Larkins, Saul Newman, Tom Henderson and Peter Reece at Goldsmiths; Judi Atkins at Aston University; and my son, Luis, to whom this book is dedicated. Parts of Chapter 4 appear in a contribution to S. Kruger, et al. *Fomenting Political Violence* (Basingstoke: Palgrave, 2018).

Introduction

Nothing gets people arguing more than argument itself. Public disagreements so frequently dissolve into acrimony over what is a permissible claim, which remarks count as fair and factual, or who is a genuine participant worthy of hearing. That is because to engage in argument is more than just to express an opinion. It is to modify the space of argument itself so that alternative opinions (and the people who hold them) are diminished or compelled to react. Argument – or, more broadly, 'rhetoric' – is an activity of speech that involves, simultaneously, expressing one's views *and* controlling opportunities for others to express their own. People bicker over the conditions of engagement because they anticipate, correctly, they might not get heard as they would prefer. We like to imagine public debate as a noble and inclusive endeavour based on respect for free expression of different opinions but, unavoidably, most arguing entails a more-or-less subtle contest for advantage. 'Speech constrains', claims Stanley Fish, 'because as an action impelled by belief and conviction it is always in the business (implicitly if not explicitly) of rejecting and stigmatising the beliefs and convictions of others' (Fish, 1999: 93. See also Fish, 2016).

What is at stake in social and political discourse, then, is rarely a matter of innocently getting one's voice heard. More than that, we affirm our stance towards a wider situation and try to get others to recognise it, even accept it as their own. That is why rhetoric matters to politics. Beyond mere self-expression, to speak and argue in public is to affect others. The way argumentative speech is formulated functions in excess of its overt propositional content and, as such, disposes auditors in more or less favourable ways towards that content. How you make your case – that is, the rhetorical strategies you adopt – inevitably figures broader interactions, enabling (as well as limiting) certain possibilities such as making new alliances or shifting altogether the focus of attention. It is the 'dispositional' quality of rhetoric, I claim in this book, that provokes and mobilises subjective commitments and aligns them to public positions. Speech, I contend, is the locus of a 'psychopolitics' whereby unconscious desires are incited and recruited by argumentative practices.

It is perhaps because of this power to dispose an audience that we are often ambivalent, if not downright suspicious, about some public discourse. The frequent, barely hidden interplay of mastery and submission – of 'winning' the argument and 'defeating' the opponent – can, for many, be highly appealing but also, for others, radically off-putting. On the one hand, we admire the eloquent and balanced vindication of a point of view. But, on the other, we recoil from what seems like rancorous disputation, dishonesty, or unseemly intransigence (especially when others appear to relish it). We may prefer to be 'rationally' persuaded but also fear that, in the other's way of arguing, we might also be deceived, compromised, or made complicit with something objectionable. Arguments of various types exert a powerful allure over people, on occasion granting them sudden analytical clarity, stirring moral righteousness, or pricking their consciences; but they can also lead them into conceptual and political traps and blind alleys that make their advocates dogmatic, offensive, or simply foolish. Public speech and debate are psychosocial practices, working at the ambiguous, occasionally risky interface of intimate inclinations and outward alignments. Propositions, reasons and observations are deployed to get 'under the skin' of listeners so as to incite and draw out their deepest, sometimes most scandalous motivations.

Think, for example, of the recent election of President Donald Trump in the US or the referendum decision to leave the European Union by voters in the UK (so-called 'Brexit'). In both instances, the language employed in these campaigns was frequently pungent and openly hostile: Trump and his supporters delighted in chanting the demand 'Lock Her Up' at his opponent, Hillary Clinton; proponents of Brexit drew upon groundless horror stories about hordes of foreigners invading the country or the magnificent ease with which the massive task of departing the EU would be accomplished. The ways voters were addressed in these extraordinary cases functioned to mislead, heighten tension, amplify prejudices and resentment ... and win acclaim! The exhortations to 'Make America Great Again', 'drain the swamp', or to 'take our country back' were crude and simplistic but tapped a deep well of resentment at established politics. This campaign rhetoric was neither especially eloquent nor subtle but it gathered sufficient support – despite all expectations – to win the day, with huge consequences in each instance. Trump's success and the marginal win for Brexit suggest that it is not merely what you say, but what is felt to be *in* what you say, that can make all the difference. Here voters found themselves rhetorically disposed to their situations in ways that excited them and dislodged any lingering attachment to alternatives. Not all speech is as scandalous as that surrounding Trump or Brexit, of course. But these examples raise the question of how public speech and argument acquires such a powerful motivating force.

Speech, I want to argue, enacts a politics of its own. It operates on the in-between ground connecting the surfaces and depths of what is felt as plausible or acceptable. In this book, I set out a way of understanding rhetoric's politics by way of the insights of psychoanalysis, especially the work of the French psychoanalytic thinker, Jacques Lacan. Psychoanalysis also enquires into an in-between space but, this time, of subjectivity, where unconscious desires rise to the surface in the form of fantasies, aberrant behaviours, and intense feelings of attachment or revulsion. A 'psychopolitics of speech' presents rhetorical strategies as ways to activate these deeper currents so as to shift the horizons of what counts as plausible, urgent, or necessary. It then asks how we might think of public discourse, not as a tool of benign rationality, but as a means to encounter and manage the powerful, sometimes menacing but also liberating, excesses that erupt into public culture.

In the rest of this introduction, I set out some of the reasons for the approach adopted in the book and anticipate the direction it takes.

Speaking Desires

My approach brings together rhetorical studies with psychoanalytic theory to reflect on how public speech seeks to activate and manage desires. In this, it is primarily a theoretical exercise aimed at making conceptual connections between the two fields. Rhetorical enquiry is traditionally concerned with the strategies and 'devices' of speech in specific situations, often with a view to grasping how speech assists (or not) in sustaining civic co-existence (see Martin, 2014). Psychoanalysis, on the other hand, is a therapeutically oriented discipline focused both on explaining the unconscious dynamics of subjective behaviour and on treating emotional illness. Where rhetoric dwells on what people consciously say and how they say it, psychoanalysis investigates how something unconscious tries to *speak through* us, frequently in spite of our explicit intentions (Frosh, 2010: 8).

In public speech we hear, to varying degrees, manifest desires intertwined with modes of discourse that restrain, qualify, or just delay their force, in order to make them palatable (to ourselves and to others). Metaphors, euphemisms, analogies or epithets, for example, are regularly employed to convey and to disguise attitudes. Connecting the fields of rhetoric and psychoanalysis means asking how speech positions its auditors on contentious matters by simultaneously expressing desires *and* repressing them. In this respect, rhetoric could be said to work in a way similar to what Freud described as a 'neurotic symptom' (see SE16: 257–72), that is, by 'knotting together' opposing strands of ambivalent feelings into a whole (Boothby, 2001: 176). Psychoanalytic symptoms emerge when we experience the discomforting torsions of unconscious urges that, because we also refuse them, find satisfaction in strange behaviours (slips of the tongue, bungled actions, phantom pains, and so on), which partially release the pressure such urges exert. So many famous speeches, for instance, draw audiences towards dramatic contrasts that simultaneously contain, release and restrain powerful sentiments. Think of Martin Luther King's memorable address in Washington of 1963, whose insistent invocation of his 'dream' of racial justice follows from a depiction of the horrific 'manacles of segregation and the chains of discrimination' (King, 1999: 328). But the enigmatic power of King's dream lies, in part, by his mediation of this contrast when, continuing the metaphor of bodily capture, he cautions his audience 'not to satisfy our thirst for freedom by drinking from the cup of bitterness and hatred' (1999: 329).

Rhetorically crafted speech – whether our own or that of those who speak for us – assembles demands in such a way as to achieve that which we cannot satisfy directly. Sometimes it is because these desires are unclear to us (such as anxiety about the future) or it is because they are obscene and therefore unacceptable (such as forms of prejudice or violence). Instead, our desires find expression by modes of argument that address them in relatively acceptable ways: for example, as humorous asides, sharply directed invective, or insistent factual analysis. Desires get spoken by way of rhetorical choices that, even if at odds with the full force and complexity of the underlying sentiment they stoke, render them appropriate for the audience or the occasion.

But rhetoric isn't merely a disguise or filter for deeper, otherwise hidden feelings. Too often rhetoric is misconceived as simply embellishing discourse, which invites us to avoid paying it serious attention as though it were a mere supplement to something else. Without *some*, even minimal, rhetorical processing, our inclinations remain inchoate and without the solidity to give them force or direction. Rhetoric formulates such feelings into determinate thoughts in the form of propositions, reasons, intellectual steps and maneuvers, or attitudes signalling our attachments or inhibitions, if only selectively and with a view to what seems appropriate given the circumstance. Which is to suggest that our attitudes and feelings never fully pre-exist speech but are, at least in part, assembled through it: to have conscious thoughts and inclinations about an issue is, typically, to eke out words to say it. Similarly, for Lacan, 'a symptom is language from which speech must be delivered' (Lacan, 2006: 223). It involves a body struggling to symbolise what cannot yet be directly spoken. In his dream analysis, claims Lacan, Freud shows that what matters most 'is given in the telling of the dream – that is, in its rhetoric', where the subject selectively assembles the dream into a discourse for the analyst (2006: 221). Psychoanalytic thinking invites us to consider that what is at work in speech concerns the constitution of human subjectivity as such. To be a person with a 'self' that discriminates one feeling or attitude from another is to participate in language and, more importantly, in argument. We feel we 'know' ourselves best usually when we can describe how we align to our world and give justification for our stance. Subjective life is thus bound up with rhetorical practice – the ongoing management of the controversy of being a self – and public discourse is the domain that the self undergoes such assemblage.

To invoke psychoanalysis, of course, isn't to just theorise subjectivity as another word for 'mind' or 'belief' but, moreover, to raise its most controversial theme: sex. For psychoanalysis, sex is the *ur*-scandal we find it most difficult to discuss. Freud's great innovation was to demonstrate how the psyche and all its dynamics are organised predominantly around the management of 'libidinal' desire. But how does this relate to the study of speech and rhetoric? Sex is a touchy issue because it concerns the largely invisible core of what it means to be a subject. For Freud, sex names not simply reproductive instincts or lustful desires but, more than that, the primary modality by which human subjects are present in, and disposed towards, the world. Sex and sexuality describe structures of psychically motivated social behaviour through which humans organise their most intimate sense of bodily constitution and attitudinal orientation. Such a sense is largely unconscious but it influences our conscious choices and perceptions, feeding into our moral frameworks, attitudes towards authority, and personal expectations of risk and reward. Speech doesn't need to be *about* sex, gender or pleasure in order to engage these primordial sensitivities. Instead, it does so indirectly by way of metaphorical associations and rhetorical gestures that I have suggested help dispose an audience by engaging their most basic structures of desire.

More than helping explain certain metaphors and gestures, however, psychoanalysis directs us to the way public discourse encircles – with varying degrees of proximity – that part of selfhood that is utterly unspeakable and beyond rational comprehension. If public discourse aims to capture attention by 'speaking desires' as if they were reasonable demands, it does so because there is something intrinsically opaque, and inaccessible, and therefore 'dangerous' that motivates them (see Wright, 1999). Speech and argument build pathways to experience our desire *as if it* were knowable and therefore satisfiable. But at the centre of subjectivity lies an impossible organic force – what Freud calls the 'drive' – that can never be sated. While the objects of our desire vary over time, humans only exist *as* desiring creatures, unable ever to achieve final and complete satisfaction. The task of speech, then, is not only to evoke desire but, further, to find ways to orient ourselves towards this uncanny, insatiable force that propels us along and, thereby, limit the threat that it poses to psychic and social order. In short, public speech aims to get a grip on this excessive part of ourselves. In so far as such discourse engages the deepest reservoirs of selfhood, it must gesture towards what is fundamentally unspeakable in the subject. For example, Trump promised 'greatness', Brexit offered total 'national sovereignty', and – a lifetime earlier – even King invoked a justice that 'rolls down like waters and righteousness like a mighty stream' (1999: 329). Such notions, which invoke a missing plenitude, invite auditors to feel the uncanny contortions of selfhood as an absent integrity that, with the right kind of determination, will actually be restored.

The approach adopted here, then, pursues the following, somewhat paradoxical, claim: individual subjects are motivated, fundamentally, not by the realisation of their desires but, rather, by their dissatisfaction (see McGowan, 2013). What moves them most deeply is not the pleasure of acquiring specific objects in life (sex, money, or power) but the loss of the privileged object that, by its very absence, promises to resolve the insatiability and opacity of desire as such. All our demands and strivings are fundamentally motivated by the urge to recover in some form this 'lost object' (see Freud, SE14: 243–58; SE18: 14–17). Freud's lesson is not that all actions have at their root the demand to satisfy a primitive sexual urge that society and its conventions prevent us from freely realising. Rather, it is that no object is ever enough to satisfy our craving and we are subsequently compelled, repeatedly, to seek out our missing source of fulfilment.

Yet psychoanalysis tells us that this lost object only exists as lost and so it can never be re-found and so never satisfied. Indeed, it is its lost quality that endows substitute objects (such as, for example, cars, lifestyles, images of social justice, or falling in love) with the alluring promise of attainable satisfaction. But once we actually acquire these things (if we can at all) they become displeasingly mundane and our search begins anew. This disappointment is constitutive of what it means to be a desiring subject. It is only by the generic absence of satisfaction that we desire in the first place. Thus it is dissatisfaction, or loss, that is the fundamental condition of subjectivity.

If public and political speech regularly points us to the many concrete sources of satisfaction and highlights the obstacles that stop us from getting them, the underlying lure is our dissatisfaction. Indeed, I want to suggest that the purpose of rhetoric is to invoke dissatisfaction and to identify obstacles, often (though by no means always) in order to indicate how they can be overcome. While we may be drawn to the objects that promise eventual satisfaction, the work of public speech and argument lies in opening up the space in which our desires come to be visible to us as unachieved. It is this space – marked out for example by reference to incomplete ideals (such as the 'promissory note' invoked by King) neglected traditions, distant future possibilities, traumas, betrayals, and so on – that particular objects (such as characters, policies, programmes or just critical dispositions) acquire distinction as a means to imagine overcoming dissatisfaction. The struggle to monopolise the space of argument, mentioned in my opening paragraph, is really a struggle over which version of dissatisfaction should rule.

But what is the appeal of dissatisfaction? Todd McGowan (2013) argues that dissatisfaction is itself strangely enjoyable (in the psychoanalytic sense of intensely, painfully absorbing) and not just because it helps 'charge up' substitute objects with feeling. For disappointment and loss, though in themselves consciously distressing, generate a powerful, if unconscious, sensation of fulfilment. But it is not a fulfilment that we can ever actually realise. It is the experience of loss itself that brings us closest to the overwhelming sense of plenitude we feel has been sacrificed. That is not to say that the objects we often talk about in public discourse are not valued but, rather, that they receive their lustre from a light cast by the experience of dissatisfaction.

Although rhetoric and speech are frequently presented as practical, problem-solving activities, they are, I want to claim, rooted in a secret dialogue with this constitutive dimension to subjectivity. That is because, as McGowan points out, language 'is the site of our founding sacrifice' (2013: 27–28). It is in acquiring language that we enter a symbolic world that severs our connection to what – from the side of language, at least – seems like a condition of blissful plenitude, often associated by psychoanalysis with the mother figure. Thus it is in language – and, I want to suggest, argument – that we repeatedly undertake to return to that founding loss at the very same time as we deal with the practical and mundane tasks of communicating and adjusting to 'real world' problems. It is not that loss and dissatisfaction somehow interrupt or prevent us from articulating practical concerns in speech but, rather, the urgency of these measures only comes into view in light of their proximity to a horizon that loss and dissatisfaction open. While speakers want their listeners to focus on the manifest goals and benefits they identify and the hurdles they need to overcome in order to achieve them, I am suggesting that rhetoricians should also focus on the latent dispositional force of loss in such discourses – the implied or explicit disjunctures, gaps, or blockages – by which dissatisfaction frames our perceptions.

The Politics of Public Affects

What benefit is there in conceiving rhetoric as a medium of desire? Political scientists frequently appeal to some intrinsic, if minimal, rational motivation to account for how people behave in organisations and institutions. But, from a psychoanalytical perspective, the internal coherence of interests or rationality is insufficient to explain how – and how intensely – subjective desire is assembled through discourse. Indeed, it is often the case – as the examples of Trump or Brexit have demonstrated – that we simply can't predict what kind of discourse will grip people sufficiently such that they rethink what their interests are and how they may best be served. Knowing one's interests or rational preferences is not the same as *wanting* to pursue them. My suggestion here is that whatever particular view comes to represent our interests, its attraction stems from its relation to a lost object that can never be represented. Such a view moves us beyond positive forms of rationality as the ground of rhetorical discourse and onto the more ambiguous terrain we associate with 'affects'.

For psychoanalysis, desire has primacy over knowledge. That is to say, the pressure of our desire exerts a more powerful force on us than that of knowing a truth. Public speech and argument has long been accused – at least in its most notorious forms – of simply pandering to people's appetites rather than dedicating itself to the pursuit of knowledge. It is for this reason that the ancient philosopher, Plato, dismissed rhetoric as a genuine art because, in dwelling on the 'how' of speech rather than the 'what', it remains fundamentally objectless and so unconstrained by any respect for knowledge. From that perspective, rhetoric is concerned merely with the process of communication and not with its ends, over which it is morally (but also perhaps cynically) neutral. But if Plato has a point in suggesting that rhetoric can be turned to any goal, moral or immoral, it is not true that it has no object. However, its object is not a substantial one but, as I have suggested, a *lost* object. Which is to say that rhetoric has the task not of merely 'telling the truth' but of putting truth into a form that makes it desirable.

King's articulation of racial justice as an extension of 'the American dream', is a case in point (see King, 1999: 330). And in this respect, psychoanalytical and rhetorical enquiry have an important and distinctive contribution to make in the understanding of affect in public culture.

The presence of what are variously termed emotions, feelings, passions or affects in politics and social life is increasingly salient in both academic and popular discourse (see Richards, 2007; Wetherell, 2012). The importance of emotions in practices of ritual, memory or popular struggles, in the media and in practices of campaigning, deliberating, or just observing politics and political activity is ever more a focus of empirical and theoretical study. Likewise, the influence of unperceived feelings and unacknowledged affects in how citizens make judgements has become a rich field for policy makers drawing from the insights of, for instance, behavioural economics or cognitive neuroscience (see Thaler and Sunstein, 2009; Marcus, 2002). Equally, much of western political culture is ever more attuned to a pervasive social media, where triggering outrage and anger as well as solidarity and conviction are now part of the daily routine of sharing opinions. Emotions and affects, it seems, are erupting everywhere and everyone appears ready to talk about them.

The growing attention devoted to emotions and affects underscores the increasingly blurred boundary separating what is perceived as 'public' and 'private' in contemporary societies. The public/private distinction will always be a matter of degree wherever politics is accountable to the people, since formal politics is charged with delivering popular wishes, incorporating them into its concerns or passing judgement on them. But new technologies (such as digital communications) and new modes of governance (such as the use of media, 'celebrity', and so on) are radically transforming the character of intimacy in public life, making it public in new ways and reminding us that the personal is never that far (if it ever was) from political contest. If democratic politics always involved the stimulation and management of feelings and emotions, in today's highly mediated and communicative capitalist democracies, we are explicitly immersed in them (see Davies, 2018; Konings, 2015).

An approach to rhetoric informed by psychoanalytic theory offers a unique way to explore the workings of affects in a world where public and private domains increasingly intertwine. Speech and argument, I want to suggest, remain among the primary means by which citizens are affectively engaged with formal and informal politics. At first this may sound absurd, especially given the widespread view that people are cynical about, perhaps even 'hate', politics and politicians (see Hay, 2007). But it is the intensity of their disregard for politics that suggests it is hard *not* to feel strongly, one way or another, about political authority and its workings. Speech is still the dominant medium through which authority is encountered by citizens, whether as governmental pronouncements, debates and arguments about policies and their moral worth, public ceremonies, media and social media commentary, or election campaigns. While most people are no longer expected patiently to hear lengthy speeches or make sophisticated judgements on public oratory, especially in world dominated by fleeting appeals to sentiment (Davies, 2018: 15–17), the constant chatter of public discourse and argumentative interchanges are nonetheless unavoidable in democratic societies. Of course, many types of public discourse increasingly adopt an entertainment dimension (such as TV news or radio debates), nonetheless all such discourse serves not merely to inform the public but offers up accessible places from which to take up, or adjust, affective positions in relation to power and authority, what it demands of them and what is demanded of it.

Speech and discourse is thus the site at which feelings, emotions and affectivity gather and mobilise popular attention. Exploring rhetoric from a psychoanalytic perspective therefore departs from some other invocations of affect, which are sometimes taken as purely material processes independent of mental life, especially language (see Angerer, 2015). For Lacan language is the primary medium of desire and it is this insistence that makes his work relevant to the study of rhetoric and speech strategies. He was himself particularly attuned to rhetorical aspects of language and their impact on subjectivity (see Lundberg, 2012). A psychoanalytic approach to rhetoric encourages us to explore how public speech strategies draw upon and interact with deeply rooted layers of subjectivity, so as to negotiate particular ways of perceiving the world and the objects in it (see Martin, 2016). Speaking is an activity that inserts elements of the personal into a public domain in the form of voices, characters and bodies, opinions and observations, by addressing others and talking of matters that concern them. In speech, the personal and intimate realms are profoundly interwoven with the social and common; but they are also transformed by them. Personal views, mannerisms and observations are magnified; they seem to become (or anticipate becoming) exemplary in some way, gestures are enlarged and invested with significance. Likewise, public matters (or those deemed to be so) are given a 'personal touch' in the form of stories and anecdotes, whether as the specific experiences of a speaker or as matters of known concern to the auditor(s). In speech, the personal is writ large and the public rendered familiar.

The affective dimensions of speech, I will claim, are rooted in a compulsion in subjectivity to recover the primordial lost object. Passionate attachments and intense hostilities present in public cultures dispose subjects towards this object by structuring desires and finding ways for people to experience their dissatisfaction. The public world is replete with debates, disagreements and arguments that express, for example, anxieties, threats and dangers, resentment and paranoia, hate and prejudice, as well as sentimental memories, traumas, and the idealisation of events and figures – a vast range of emotions, feelings and affective states that attach to and are conveyed, momentarily, via controversies that characterise our shared loss.

Chapter Outline

How then do I propose to explore the psychopolitics of speech? The book develops a line of theoretical enquiry through the work of Lacan but it is not a full exposition of his ideas nor, I hope, a forbidding, self-consciously 'Lacanian' enterprise. Such efforts can often be heavy-going and my preference, instead, has been to set out an accessible way of thinking about rhetoric that draws selectively upon, rather than devotes itself to elaborating in detail, Lacan's insights. More technical readings or specialist applications can certainly be found elsewhere (see, for example: Lundberg, 2012; Solomon, 2015; Millar, 2006). As I have implied above, Lacan alerts us to the place of desire in structuring subjectivity and, moreover, to the way desire exceeds any secure form of containment. In the chapters that follow, I explore what this means and how it connects to certain rhetorical themes. Below, let me summarise in more detail the positions developed in each chapter.

Chapter 1 opens by raising the question of the 'subject' of speech. I invite the reader to consider speaking not just as a medium for the transmission of thought but as an activity of organising one's bodily connection to the wider world. The subject, then, is not merely a conscious mind but a body actively constituting its world, managing the resistances it meets and mobilising its energies accordingly. In modern times, the division between 'mind' and 'body', and the wider separation of politics from society, has certainly diminished our receptivity to the corporeal dimensions of speech. Against this tendency I draw upon the work of phenomenologist Maurice Merleau-Ponty to begin to rethink speech as a manifestation of an embodied subjectivity. In particular, I underscore the value of his concept of the 'flesh' as a suggestive way to conceive of rhetoric as a carnal practice that stimulates and coordinates, reveals and conceals, our perceptual attentions.

In Chapter 2, I turn at last to psychoanalysis and begin to explore Lacan's theory of the subject. The key insight of psychoanalysis, I suggest, lies in understanding the conflicts that assail social orders as being anchored in a fundamental division within subjectivity that both incites its desire but also thwarts it. Human subjects are, consequently, inclined to identify with 'plausible stories' that protect them from this otherwise painful condition of division. Lacan's contribution to psychoanalytical theory, I explain, emerges from his distinction between the subject's three registers (the imaginary, the symbolic and the real) and the impossible closure brought by their interaction. He offers a compelling account of how the subject seeks to make coherent its relation to the world by the mediation of 'the Other' – a symbolic figure simultaneously inside and outside the subject, invoked by language – which coordinates its desire around a lost enjoyment it can never redeem.

Chapter 3 deepens the exploration of Lacan's work by elaborating his account of signification and fantasy. Here I draw upon Richard Boothby's reading of Lacan's theory of the subject as an account of perceptual organisation where a world is disclosed by way of processes of 'position' and 'disposition'. Fantasy is thus understood as a means to enable the subject to position itself inside a horizon of meaning by investing its excess in the image of a lost object that disposes it towards its horizons. The importance of fantasy to public speech and political rhetoric, I argue, therefore lies in figuring this horizon and enabling subjects to manage their desire by way of loss. Lacan's notion of a lost object – conceived via the figure of the *objet petit a*, the so-called 'object cause of desire' – underscores a distinctively visual dimension to rhetoric and reframes the notion of the 'rhetorical situation' accordingly.

In Chapter 4, I direct the approach developed thus far towards the theme of vituperation and hatefulness in public speech. Verbal insults, 'hate speech' and aggressive discourse generally are interesting because they can be conceived as sublimations of the violence that speech is often believed to eliminate. The 'bitter argument' – that is, speech aimed not at constructively building social bonds or cultivating positive, inclusive relations but, instead, at promoting exclusion, division and discomfort – is more common in public discourse than we are often prepared to admit. It is because it exhibits an explicit and direct discharge of energy that it is, in its own way, tremendously gratifying, despite being routinely disavowed. Rather than dismiss it out of hand, however, I suggest we regard vituperation as symptomatic of the way social discourse and political argument police the 'sacrifice' of enjoyment upon which civil bonds depend. To illustrate my point I note some of the arguments around the presence of anti-semitism in the British Labour Party in recent years.

The question of what an ethical approach to public speech might look like is the topic of Chapter 5. Rhetoric has always been associated, if only implicitly, with an ancient notion of virtue conceived as the underlying cement of the just order: instructing citizens to speak well in order to promote shared ends. But such a notion is premised on the view that society coheres around a concept of the sovereign good. In the approach presented in this book, however, such a society is unattainable. The attraction of the good lies in its absence, not its presence. We are motivated towards the good only because it is perceived to be lost or prohibited. An 'ethics of speech', according to Lacan's account of psychoanalytic ethics, consists not in the alignment of speech with an idea of the good but, rather, in grasping its absence as the very condition for our desire. For speech to be ethical in this sense, I claim, means not to insist on prohibiting desire by aligning with the Other but, rather, to understand the limits of our being as internally rather than externally constituted. To illustrate the point, I look to the rhetorics of polemic and testimony as examples of how to incorporate loss into ethical speech dispositions.

Such a view, I want to suggest, invites a rhetorical culture that is *not* slavishly tailored to the prohibitions of a current or imagined social order but, instead, to sustaining difference and disagreement, controversy and disputation as the key to sharing a common world. Only by incorporating an awareness of the primacy of loss and dissatisfaction in rhetorical cultures, I note in the Conclusion, can we confidently submit ourselves to what I call 'the flesh of argument'.

1. Bodies of Speech

Who is the 'subject' of speech? We are accustomed to imagining speech as the emanation of an individual's mind: a package of thoughts representing some prior cogitation. To speak is, accordingly, to 'say what you think', suggesting a coincidence between the exterior voice and some interior agency motivating it. Persuasive speech, on this account, entails assembling one's thoughts into a 'message' honed to appeal to other minds. While such a view describes some situations (such as expressing an opinion), nonetheless it doesn't account for how, sometimes, we prefer to let others speak for us, or how we adopt words and phrases only for certain situations and not others, or even how we frequently find ourselves saying things we don't really mean. Instead of saying what we think, very often we just let the words do the talking. In this chapter I make some initial reflections on the relation of speech to subjectivity and suggest that, in rhetorical enquiry, speech might usefully be conceived as a medium of *embodied* subjects rather than purely self-conscious or calculating minds isolated from their social and material environments. An embodied notion of the subject emphasises the layers of corporeal experience – not all of it conscious – that conjoins subjects to the worlds they inhabit and help constitute. In turn, speech can be conceived less as an intellectual activity and, more expansively, as a medium to adjust and coordinate our perceptual and emotional responses to the world. In later chapters, this fashioning of a world will be explored in terms of the movement and organisation of 'desire'.

In recent years, the relationship between language and embodiment has been a topic of debate among philosophers and social theorists. Many have come to argue that thought extends beyond the inner space of the mind and is closely bound up with bodies, affects, and 'materiality' (see Poynton and Lee, 2011). But how might these insights be relevant to the study of rhetoric? To consider speech as part of a bodily subjectivity is not to substitute its conceptual element for a purely material one but, rather, to focus on the intermingling of the two realms. Speech always involves sensation as well as sense; it 'folds', 'cuts' and 'articulates' meaning with feeling (MacKendrick, 2004: 91–114). A rhetorical enquiry directed at this intermingling attends to the way speech works to 'incarnate' a world, activating layers of corporeality rather than merely sending information. To grasp this requires us to set aside the abstract subject of modernity – which experiences its perception in isolated sensations – and think of the subject and its rhetorical activity as movements affecting other bodily subjects, frequently by alerting them to their own limits: that is, by shifting weight, investing force and giving orientation, concealing and revealing, connecting and dividing, and so on. Speech might fruitfully be thought of as a form of touching from a distance; stimulating and quelling emotions, and putting audiences 'in touch' with their priorities.

In what follows, I give only an initial indication of the elements of this kind of approach. To do so, I draw upon the work of the phenomenologist Maurice Merleau-Ponty. His interpretation of the body as the site of a primordial perceptual engagement offers important insights for thinking about rhetorical sense-making in corporeal rather than narrowly cognitive terms. Although I don't stick to his mode of analysis in the rest of the book, nonetheless Merleau-Ponty's notions of the 'body-subject' and, in particular, the 'flesh' shift attention from mental to corporeal qualities of subjectivity. This will pave the way for my later discussion of speech as the activation of the psyche.

The Body in Motion

The body is the hidden underside of political discourse. Although speech is so clearly a practice of the body – in that it takes the physical apparatus of a voice to speak, lungs to project, ears to hear and so on – its corporeal dimensions almost entirely recede from attention when we are actually engaged in doing it. We focus, instead, on what is being *talked about*. Of course, we probably note in passing a speaker's accent, the timbre of their voice, even the selection of certain words, gestures, or emphases and variations in pace. But, unlike singing for example, if we are listening properly these textures will mostly fade from immediate attention. Even less do we notice the qualities of our own voices. To engage in speech is not to attend to its immediate physicality but to direct ourselves beyond it, to anticipate and register the ongoing making of sense. Speech, we could say, only works because the medium of the body is perceptually diminished. Its signifying function depends on our implicit agreement not to be distracted unduly by any sensual qualities.

But the body is never entirely erased. Rather, it is rendered feint. Even though we withdraw our attention, public speech requires bodies to be present, attentive, and subtly receptive to changes in volume, tone and emphasis, as well as to react and respond to what is heard. Although some (such as Mark Zuckerberg, founder of *Facebook*) fantasise of a voiceless communication that can be transmitted telepathically – thereby bypassing the external body – till now, making and hearing speech remains an unavoidably corporeal activity (see Yadron, 2016; Davies, 2018: 176–8). The body is therefore both present and absent in public discourse, both a necessary and yet unacknowledged condition of almost all communication. The effect of this is to give speech a strangely 'virtual' quality that allows it to transcend the constraints of its circumstances: it is both somewhere and nowhere at once, a situated voice in time and space, a sound emitting from a particular body to a particular audience, and yet transmitting meanings that are irreducible to the circumstances of their production. Both intimate and public, inside and outside our heads, evaporating contingently in real time and yet inscribed silently into memory, often precise but always revisable; speech neither fully attaches to, nor separates from, the bodies that produce or hear it.

Yet it may be this uncanny virtuality to discourse, the way it emerges from but never clings wholly to human bodies, that accounts for its powerful effects. It is because speech gestures beyond the here and now that it can open up a world, a space beyond the immediate situation, signifying not just contingent concerns but assembling a context, or 'horizon', inside which such matters acquire relative significance and value. Moreover, speech permits us to modify the space of an encounter, to position ourselves anew towards matters and each other in ways that our bodies in themselves cannot. That way, bodies are released from fixed determination and ushered into an incipient condition, projecting themselves into a domain outside their immediate presence. Yet because bodies are so profoundly involved, if not foregrounded, in this making of meaning, the world that is signified is never wholly separable from its context, addressees or the stance of the speaker(s). Just as the revelation of bad news or bitter confrontations can leave unpleasant atmospheres in their wake, speech frequently remains tangled in the residues of its enunciation. Whatever we talk about or argue for, however abstract or directed to the future, it is always inflected by the conditions of the moment, the style of the speaker, prevailing urgencies and tensions, and so forth.

There is, I want to suggest, an unacknowledged complicity of bodies and speech: bodies give speech determinacy, rooting its significations in a specific location. But, like some invisible fluid, speech releases bodies from wholesale determination. In this interplay of determinacy and indeterminacy, relative closure and openness, arises the possibility of rhetoric. For rhetoric concerns the employment of speech and other symbols so as to modify the shared reception of a situation or circumstance. It allows bodies to interact figuratively, as more than just physical objects, and thereby alter their orientations, soften their hostilities or make firm their affections and alliances. The manipulation of language and meaning, for which rhetoric is well known, is thus related to the body, not merely as a register of its inner condition but as a constantly sliding surface that simultaneously reveals and conceals, asserts and revises its dispositions. That way, speakers can transform the space of interaction between bodies, bringing them into alignment or dissolving their evident solidity or homogeneity. To hear speech, to be addressed directly or indirectly, is to be exposed to the probing force of the other, compelled to respond to its terms and so figure one's own disposition and resources in return.

It is the peculiar, transitive quality of the human body – its capacity to signify one position but to gesture its motion to another – that may even be at the root of the historic suspicion of rhetoric. For speech can as easily dissemble as reveal orientation: we can always say one thing but do another. Politicians are 'oily' or 'slippery' because they make this flexibility their art. The speaking body occupies a strange 'in-between' zone where it cannot easily be defined as fully in one position or another. As Roberto Esposito argues, the body has never managed to be exhaustively conceived in Western law as either animate 'person' or inanimate 'thing' because it 'protrudes into both categories' (2015: 103). The body is often designated as continuous with personhood but the two are never wholly coincident since the person remains an abstract entity who may even sell or lose the powers of its body. Yet nor is the body fully a thing, or separable object in the world, since it remains, to a significant extent, physically conjoined to a subject and hence inviolable in a way that other objects are not. In philosophical discourse, this 'ambiguous' in-between status is even more pronounced (Marzano, 2007: 4–6). The body is both subject *and* object; and yet not fully either. In modern thought since René Descartes, who famously distinguished between the 'mind' and 'body' as two radically distinct 'substances', subjectivity is the source of cognitive certainty while the body is material extension in space. In fact, Descartes takes up the ancient dualism, originally offered by Plato, of an eternal soul imprisoned in the contingency of the body (Marzano: 2007: 16). This view supports the notion of the body as something to be mastered by consciousness, an external shell that is, fundamentally, manipulable by the abstract subject within it and so amenable to its demands. Such is the basis of modern science, which itself has taught us to control the body by treating it as another part of the material world that can bend to our will.

But in relegating the body to the material exterior, science and modern thought generally have emphasised the conceptual over the material, purifying thought and conceptuality of their intertwinement with the body and the wider world. By consequence, the ways that speech and meaning resonate with corporeal sensation and vital energies not captured wholly by consciousness has been occluded. As is so frequently highlighted by feminists, the most obvious cost of this has been the enforcement of a hierarchy of sexual difference, where women are designated as in some way more closely aligned with nature and hence further separated than men from the capacity for conceptual reasoning. Women have come to be defined by their bodies and the functions of childbirth, for example. Moreover, women are routinely sexualised, typically by reducing their value to that of external appearance. Women's exclusions from public life often used to be justified by reference to the emotions their bodies 'held over' them, whereas men were assumed to be superior in separating off their minds from their bodies and the environment (see Grosz, 1994). For that reason, among others, women have rarely been welcomed as equal participants as speakers in public and political assemblies. Their voices were (and continue to be) ridiculed as shrill, distracting, or prone to interruption by 'hysterical' emotions that get the better of them.

The body, then, is the hidden underside of political discourse not merely in the sense that speech always projects beyond its corporeal immediacy so as to make sense but, moreover, because obscuring its bodily foundation simultaneously influences the encounters through which bodies subsequently affect each other. Speech disposes bodies affectively by motioning them in different ways, naming and directing their energies, exposing them to certain experiences while shielding them from others. It puts into play, in a highly selective way, the capacity of the body to register and make sense of sensation. While we are typically concentrated on the 'ideational' content of public and political debates – the description and characterisation of certain circumstances, the practical intentions or effects of policies, the attitudes taken up by individuals around these – woven into this are layers of discourse through which speakers and auditors adjust their attentions by attending to the 'weight' of evidence or attuning themselves to their own 'grip' on a matter. These layers, which in practice seem inseparable from the things we talk about, are where we find circulating the bodily energies and impulses that undergird our public commitments.

Rhetorical action, I want to claim, draws upon this unacknowledged intermingling of bodies and speech. The body is not just a neutral, physical apparatus that transmits or receives abstract information. It is a medium that both enables and constrains the possibility of discursive interaction. In treating rhetoric as essentially conceptual practices and arrangements of abstract thought processes, we neglect the way both speaking and thinking access and articulate layers of corporeal existence. How, then, are we to understand this interrelation between rhetoric, speech and corporeality? It will help to look either side of modern thought, that is, to contexts where mind and body are not so sharply separated and consciousness is not treated as the frictionless centre of human subjectivity. As we shall see, in ancient societies, speech was already understood as an embodied practice akin to the performance of physical combat. In more recent perspectives – particularly in the work of phenomenology – the body connects language and speech to a rich 'flesh' of sensual possibilities outside of conscious experience.

Wrestling for Words

Our reception of political speech today is conditioned by a number of historical factors, of which two are worth underscoring. First is the modern 'disincorporation' of politics in western society. Individual bodies are no longer the supreme focus of public power and authority, though they remain significant. With the decline of medieval Kingship, public power ceases to centre on a single, sacred personage or clique entrusted to embody the social order (see Lefort, 1988; Santner, 2011). Political leaders now derive their authority largely from 'representing' the abstract body of 'the people' rather than by personally embodying a sacred substance. Second, the secular cultural 'disenchantment' of the world and the philosophical separation of mind and body have relocated personhood in the interiority of private conscience rather than in a wider community or unified cosmos. Under these conditions, we tend to treat speech either as the function of a formally neutral public order or, alternatively, as the expression of personal opinion. While there is undoubtedly a lot of room between these poles for different types of speech, modern conditions have made it hard to appreciate this in-between space.

The ancient tradition of rhetoric, however, long preceded these peculiarly modern conditions. Bodies were then at the centre of public life and speech was a medium for sharing in that life, not the mere expression of personal opinion. In classical Greece and Rome, rhetoric was a practice not simply of 'saying what you think' but of embodying one's argument through a performance that demonstrated attachment to a common cause. Public speech was thus 'embodied' in a number of key respects: it was always 'live' oratory, a performance of skill and resourcefulness aimed at impressing an immediate audience; and it sought to fashion and sustain the common body of the polis. Public and political argument involved securing a confluence of opinion, performed via the bodies and styles of individual orators. Ancient societies were both highly collective and highly individualistic at the same time, the competitive individual seeking to occupy the locus of communal aspirations, becoming an exemplary body on which the admiration and aspirations of the whole order might be invested.

In her *Bodily Arts* (2004) Debra Hawhee explores the close connections between rhetoric and athletics in ancient Athenian society. Public speech, she argues, was understood then as a performative practice that displayed similar kinds of skill and training as did athletics. As a civic pedagogy aimed at cultivating effective performances, rhetorical education was on a continuum with physical instruction. The aim was not to enable one simply to express oneself but to make evident one's 'bodily *aretē*' (or excellence), that is, a readiness for a contest in which speed, agility and flexibility were outward markers of virtue. Indeed 'virtue' and 'virtuosity' – moral value and skill – were viewed in Athens as broadly aligned. Virtue, in this sense, did not signify a quality that one inherently *is* but something one enacts in one's movements before an audience (Hawhee, 2004: 17–22). Whereas in athletics the contest produces a winner, in the *agon* (or contest) of public oratory the point is to display a similar type of excellence, regardless of outcome: 'What matters for *aretē* then, is not the victory per se but rather the hunt for the victory' (2004: 23).

Hawhee demonstrates fascinating parallels in both lexicon and technique between the ancient Greek training of bodies for athletics (primarily the popular sport of wrestling) and the training of speech. Each involved cultivating not abstract truths and precepts but, rather, *mētis* – a wily, 'intelligent ability' of the body – to move resourcefully in the situation at hand drawing upon immanent, rather than transcendent, principles so as to attend to emergent, unpredictable opportunities (2004: 44–64). Each involved rigid forms of training based on repetition and recall so as to discipline one's reactions and embed them in 'muscle memory', making them automatic rather than conscious. Like athletics, then, rhetorical education required the incorporation of skills as 'pre-cognitive' responses to enable the speaker to move swiftly and to evade attack as the moment allowed. Rhetorical encounters displayed one's capacity for fluent movement, to avoid being trapped, and an ability to improvise in given circumstances. This was not something one could simply learn *about* – the trainer in both rhetoric and athletics aimed not so much to impart information but to render the trainee supple and alert, ridding his body (often by its exposure to pain) of obstacles to its capacity to react (2004: 86–108). The language of rhetorical knowledge, especially in the law courts, was thus permeated by terms shared with athletics that implied corporeal readiness and dexterity: for example, the notion of 'taking a stance' *(stasis)*, 'making the weaker case the stronger', attention to timeliness *(kairos)*, and so on.

Although rhetoric was later recast as an intellectual activity by figures such as Aristotle – who famously presented it as a 'counterpart to dialectic', or philosophy – the picture presented by Hawhee suggests a practice organised not strictly around fixed conceptual principles but, rather, an acute attention to the body's capacity for contest and movement. It is not abstract truth – with statically 'eternal' ideas from which to reason – that reigns here but, rather, the ability to adapt to the challenge, to flex and to avoid being 'pinned down' by one's opponent, to intensify or release at the right moments. The athletic body and the speaking body were both trained to manoeuvre, to shift weight and transform posture in a dynamic encounter.

In this respect, argumentative encounters are less mental processes than figurative movements which are simultaneously physical *and* mental: evading capture and capitalising on the opponent's weaknesses. Mind and body are inseparable in these manoeuvres, which amount to a kind of bodily thinking that occurs without deep reflection because focused on active contest. Persuasive action is not a primarily intellectual labour of interrogating logical principles but a more encompassing activity of incarnating the audacious movements of sense so as to effectively reposition auditors. Such a view is consonant with a predominantly agonistic culture, where military, athletic and rhetorical skills are understood as parallel activities, each displaying virtue and virtuosity. In such a culture, individuals compete to present themselves as exemplars incarnating communal virtues. The body is more than the outer shell of a person (who is always male) but, instead, a disciplined blend of skills that exemplify the competitive disposition assumed of the polis in general.

Of course, it is precisely this bodily dimension to rhetoric that the philosopher, Plato, took as the sign of its moral degeneracy. Speech without the guidance of rigorous ideas and their ideal essences, in his view, was aimed at merely stimulating base pleasures and fears – bodily dispositions of a 'lower' type. So rhetoric is dismissed in his

Gorgias as a form of 'pandering' or, like fancy cookery, playing only to the audience's sensation rather than adhering to truth: a tendency that led to government by deception rather than criticality and integrity. The bodily dimension of rhetoric, argued Plato, was precisely what discredited it since bodies were merely contingent containers of an eternal soul. Only a discourse directed at transcendent ideas – understood as essentially independent of bodily forms – could rise above the transient, sensual orientation of rhetoric. That type of discourse was, of course, philosophy (see Ballacci, 2018).

But the notion that public speech was always more than an intellectual activity persisted and found further expression in the work of the great Roman lawyer, rhetorician and orator, Marcus Tullius Cicero. Although Cicero acknowledged the vital importance of reason and truth in civil affairs, his conception of rhetoric remained attached to the view that the virtues of oratory arose not from intellect alone but from bodily performance. Politics was a practice in which the orator took upon himself the burden of mediating the different orientations and values of the political community. Public speech was a political act because, through it, the speaker was challenged to incarnate the values of the polis *and* demonstrate the congruence of any claims to knowledge with those values. The good philosopher by necessity is a 'good orator', able to express passion so as to shape reason into a form that sustains the virtues of the republic.

In Cicero's *De Oratore*, for example, the ideal citizen is cultivated not merely through the training of mind but through the body as a whole. Cicero's attention is thus often on the physical body of the orator: the gestures, posture, movement and voice – all the elements that help discipline the body and permit a balanced, fluid interplay of reason and emotion. That way, the skilled orator arouses passions in his audience, provoking in them sensations and experiences that activate shared traditions and sentiments. It is that need to connect to the audience, to recruit their passions into his performance that for Cicero ties the orator to his civic duty. As Joy Connolly (2007: 139–141) argues, the orator's speaking body functions in Cicero's rhetorical theory as the 'performative' enactment of the community, signifying in various ways the positions, values, customs and reactions of Roman society, blending them into a whole. Cicero attends not only to the elements of physical delivery (or *actio*) that amplify or vary the orator's tone and intensity but also to the need in rhetorical training to rehearse competing arguments – or the method of *controversia*. To argue from 'both sides' of an issue *(in utramque partem)* and even to incorporate alternative views into one's own argument enabled speakers to acknowledge differences of opinion by embodying disputation (see Mendelson, 1998).

As Connolly acknowledges, Cicero's idealised orator is 'laden with internal contradiction' – the speaker must have specialist knowledge but appeal to popular sentiment, arouse passions but pursue rational persuasion. And he must learn to manage his own excesses and passions so as to elevate the republic to the forefront of his mind and body. Nonetheless, however unrealistic, this underscores the continued sense in ancient rhetoric that 'the operations of speech are meaningless without the accompanying presence of authentically felt passion' (Connolly, 2007: 157).

What are we to make of these bodily references in classical rhetoric? It suggests that rhetoric originates not simply as knowledge of how effectively to express one's inner thoughts but, rather, as a broader practice that draws upon speech's physical embodiment to *actively make* sense. The possibilities of the body – its capacity for movement, contortion, for physically shifting weight from one place to another – are figurative possibilities for speech. Words have athletic qualities in so much as they mirror the movements (the repetitions, reflex actions, reversals and evasions) of the body, and bodies have word-like functions in that they enable emphasis, intensification, and contest. These are always men's bodies, of course; women's bodies, like their voices, are refused entry to this homoerotic world and femininity as such is treated only with disdain (see Saxonhouse, 1992; Beard, 2017). But in their intermingling of speech and body, words are released from fixed moorings and participate in a dynamic of transformation, controlling force to figure firm positions on an issue. Speech is not a mere expression of abstract thought but the wrestling of sense into a secure stance. So when speech acts rhetorically, it acts both with and against the resistances of other embodied forces, compelling inventive and resourceful responses.

This way of making sense fits, of course, with an ancient world where the individual, male body is the unavoidable point of exposure to the vicissitudes of a competitive, precarious and often violent social order. Words and bodies were the available surfaces that mediated such exposure and so it is perhaps not surprising that the arts that refine and discipline them share a common understanding of their craft. But that way of looking at rhetoric also invites an alternative to the intellectual emphasis that we have inherited from the philosophies of Plato and Aristotle. An 'embodied rhetoric' implies that public speech has an unavoidably visceral edge to it, an underlying inclination towards physical competitiveness and passion – that is, dimensions of discourse that are not always fair or kind but, occasionally, rudely corporeal, where the energies of the body may on occasion overwhelm the subtleties of sense. Of course, this edge is disavowed in a philosophically oriented rhetoric that seeks conceptual order and intellectual coherence so as to produce societies that are the same. But the alternative, based upon the model of wrestling and competitive sport, reminds us that public speech is often only a means to displace or manage the threat of violence, to discipline it rather than eliminate it altogether, so as to work its force to less damaging ends.

In the modern world, however, bodies are significantly diminished as the privileged medium of public power and authority. Rendered increasingly 'immune' by the structures of the modern state from the dangers and violence to which their ancient ancestors were exposed, modern citizens need not fundamentally rely on their military or political allegiances to survive (see Esposito, 2008). Sacred status can no longer be claimed by a leader in a secular world and thus no figure may fully incarnate communal order – either by a display of military or political prowess or by evidence of royal lineage. As Ernesto Laclau puts it, the 'logic of incarnation' has been 'interrupted' in modernity (Laclau, 1996: 23). No individual body is assigned intrinsic or unlimited right to power. Instead, politics gradually comes to be conducted as a (relatively) peaceful competition to 'represent' (or incarnate only temporarily) the wider social body conceived abstractly – the nation, the people, the workers, and so on. Of course, bodies remain vital to politics – in democratic assemblies, civil associations, social struggles and political conflicts – but often as resources for organisation and objects of discipline. The focus of public rhetoric becomes much more abstract ('the good of the people') and its sources ever more widely rooted in everyday, rather than a restricted or elite, language and experience.

But the greater transparency of politics in modern society, the increased accountability of its personnel to the rule of law, and its relative openness to the concerns of ordinary people, nonetheless all come at a cost. The more bodies that are seen and voices heard, the less certain we are as to what principles unify them. Bodies remain strangely opaque, despite their abundant presence in public life, and thus a source of ever more doubt and anxiety. Deprived of intrinsic communal significance, bodies come to be viewed as material to be studied, interpreted or ruled over. Our knowledge of them becomes abstract, classificatory, moralising, rather than situated or sympathetic. We are attuned to their 'aberrant' tendencies and our capacity to 'improve' them. Michel Foucault's notion of 'biopolitics' – whereby the 'health' and habits of whole populations are increasingly subject to expert analysis and intervention – underscores precisely the modern obsession with bodies as a suspect, unknown material to be worked upon for social purposes (see Foucault, 2008).

In order better to grasp the rhetorical significance of corporeality today, we need to steer around the modern objectification of bodies produced by political disincorporation and the dualism of mind and body. In the next section I explore one way we might retrieve the body's presence in subjectivity and thereby rethink its relation to public speech.

Merleau-Ponty and the Lived Body

The modern reception of rhetoric, I have suggested, is premised on an assumed dualism separating the mental from the material, ideas from 'reality', or subject from object. Speech is so often presumed to have an obligation to mirror or represent faithfully a world that is fundamentally separate from it. While there are, undoubtedly, good grounds for acknowledging this division – not least that it allows us to be sceptical of truth claims and the power they can mobilise if uncritically accepted – when taken as a cardinal principle, it obscures what else is going on in speech by relegating it to the realm of passive subjectivity. Treating speech as representation, it assumes there is already a perceptible world 'out there' and so elides the ways we are actively involved in constituting it. But to 'constitute' the world is not merely to impose ideas upon it, to smother it in 'discourse' any which way we choose, but, rather, to engage it corporeally.

For Maurice Merleau-Ponty it is the human body as a whole that perceives and not some inner consciousness located in the brain. In his *Phenomenology of Perception* (2012) he refused the modern prejudice that human subjects either register sensations from reality or impose their concepts on the flux of experience. Perception, in his view, is very far from a passive reception of discrete sensations from the external environment, channeled through the senses and the nervous system to the brain. Rather, perception involves the active engagement of the body in its lived comportment within an environment. Only subsequently do we break down experience into separate processes and atomistic units of sensation. For phenomenology generally, we never just receive a stream of sensations but, rather, are actively directed towards objects (both empirical and conceptual) in what is described as 'intentional experience' (Husserl, 2012: 67–8. See also Sartre, 2013). That is, consciousness perpetually seizes upon some objects rather than others, its attention always being directed to somewhere or something, focusing on one object while inattentive to others. For Merleau-Ponty, however, this active intentionality is a condition of the lived body – or what he calls the 'body-subject' – rather than consciousness alone.

Drawing upon Husserl's distinction between *der Körper* (the body as a material object) and *der Leib* (the lived body of experience) Merleau-Ponty underscores the 'pre-reflective' relation of the lived body to its world: we apprehend our environment as part of a largely unacknowledged directedness at things around us. We move within physical space and adjust our comportment to its contours or improvise without the constant prompt of consciousness. We walk along paths, turn to observe things in our view, address our attention to certain items and handle them carefully, before putting them back and continuing our walk – all without attending to each and every physical movement, sensation, choice of posture or adjustment of our hands. It is this underlying layer of pre-linguistic bodily contact – which Merleau-Ponty now defines as perception – whereby we rely unreflectively upon habits, skills and an implicit but always revisable knowledge of the environment that, for him, functions as the ground of all cognitive activity. But where cognitive judgements divide the world into discrete parts, our bodies function through a perceptual 'field' that gives tacit coherence to experience by constantly setting the objects we encounter against a wider contextual horizon that makes them implicitly meaningful (2012: 4, 50–51). Our bodies spatialise and temporalise our existence, bringing degrees of coherence to the way we inhabit a wider environment (Coole, 2007b: 415). Thus the body is the ultimate horizon of our experience, the 'pivot of the world' as he puts it, upon which all subsequent meaning ultimately depends: 'in this sense I am conscious of the world by means of my body' (2012: 84). Whereas conscious awareness attends largely to isolated experiences, our bodies are permanently engaged in rich and layered ways with its textures, zones, openings, resistances, and other sensations that are never fully captured in immediate cognition and so often overflow its registrations.

For Merleau-Ponty, it is not that we (as independent subjects) just *have* bodies. Rather, we *are* our bodies. We do not exist as isolated consciousnesses housed in material 'shells'; subjectivity simply *is* receptivity to objectivity. My 'inner world' is the chair I sit on, the bicycle I ride, the view I see, or the tools I employ. Neither subject nor object exists in isolation from the other. They intertwine in a common 'milieu' (Alloa, 2017: 23–28), swapping places at times as our bodies themselves become objects, perhaps when they falter and need attention or even fixing. But when they work again, they are part of us as a whole. So for Merleau-Ponty, who also draws upon the work of Martin Heidegger, perception implies 'being-in-the-world', or having a preconscious familiarity with objects and an implicit sense of their unity and amenability to our purposes (2012: 81–82). The body-subject opens onto a meaningful totality with an implicit normativity that guides us where we ought to go and steers away from where we shouldn't. 'My organism', he claims, 'is not like some inert thing, it sketches out the movement of existence' (2012: 86). Only when we accidentally trip on our path or find ourselves suddenly obstructed do we adjust or bring our conscious reasoning into play. But even these interruptions are experienced precisely *as* interruptions because our body implicitly 'knows' already what it wants to do – that is to say, it already inhabits a meaningful world through which it comports itself and in which it can improvise. Our world (of walking along paths) may be temporarily disordered but we are able to bring it back again, rebalancing our bodies to their intentions.

The implications of Merleau-Ponty's phenomenology of the body are profound. He decentres consciousness by claiming that human experience is irreducible to cognitive activity. Instead, consciousness is one aspect of the body's overall capacity to engage its world intentionally. By consequence, all intellectual activities presuppose and are reliant upon the possibilities occasioned by the body, even as they reach out beyond them. Our ability to reason and imagine, for example, are expressive skills rooted in bodily perspectives (see Landes, 2013). These are always spatially and temporally situated rather than objectively 'universal' perspectives. Indeed, universalism implies an impossible 'view from nowhere', as though we could see from all angles at once. Our conceptualisations presuppose spatial proximity to objects that discloses them as useful or not for certain purposes. These objects – such as clothes, walking sticks or vehicles – are barely distinguishable from our subjectivity; as the architecture of our bodily motility they are part of us and part of how we feel as we move through space. The world is therefore always 'ambiguous' to us, argues Merleau-Ponty, because we never experience it all at once from one utterly transparent perspective. Rather it is 'unveiled' only from certain angles that disclose some possibilities rather than others. We read our perspectives onto perceptual horizons that supply them only an anticipated coherence and stability. And our perspectives may become 'sedimented' in a shared, intersubjective world of customs and habits – or what the later Husserl called a 'lifeworld' – such that we forget they are perspectives at all.

It is this perspectivism of the body – its situatedness in time, place and circumstance – that suggests its connection to speech and, I also want to argue, rhetoric. For Merleau-Ponty, speech is not a categorically distinct activity – an 'external accompaniment of thought' (2012: 182) – but, rather, a specialisation of bodily expression (see Alloa, 2017: 35–57). Language, in his view, is inextricably bound up with the body's perceptual activity. For him, it originates as a kind of 'gesturing' that supports the body and its orientations. Speech, at least at its most primordial level, is functional for coordinating the body in its location and direction. Signs and symbols derive from their role in enabling positioning and movement, guiding bodies across obstacles, anticipating what is oncoming, testing textures and flavours. Many of our mundane communicative exchanges are still embedded in this world of signalling intentions, acknowledgements, comfort and discomfort, which enables us to move and adjust physically and emotionally in a world we largely take for granted. But even our 'higher-level' communications, when we devote conscious and detailed attention to what we are trying to say, function along similar corporeal 'schemes': pointing out choices about where to devote attention, highlighting risky consequences, developing balanced and secure orientations towards the matter at hand. All these symbolic formulations presuppose and cleave towards an underlying correlate of bodily comportment and perceptual integrity.

To Merleau-Ponty it is mistaken to treat thought and expression as entirely separate. We do not fully think a thought prior to expressing it in language. Rather, 'speech accomplishes thought' (2012: 183). Language imposes a temporary order on thinking, assembles it in a form such that it becomes perceptible to us as a thought with a discrete shape. Speech and language are not representations or mere verbal 'containers' of entirely premeditated cognition but formulations that 'complete' perception in a concrete expression. So language is always necessary in order to make us aware of our experience: 'the most familiar object appears indeterminate so long as we have not remembered its name [...] the thinking subject himself is in a sort of ignorance of his thoughts so long as he has not formulated them for himself' (2012: 182–3). This implies that speech is a necessary part of the way the world is corporeally engaged. Speech is a kind of perceptual thinking of the body. As Merleau-Ponty puts it:

> We must first recognize that, for the speaking subject, thought is not a representation; that is, thought does not explicitly posit objects or relations. The orator does not think prior to speaking, nor even while speaking; his speech is his thought (2012: 185).

To hear speech, then, is to have an immediate relation to the perception of an other – the way the other inhabits its world – and not merely to hear a report on the other's thoughts. 'I do not perceive the anger or the threat as a psychological fact hidden behind the gesture, I read the anger in the gesture. The gesture does not *make me think* of anger, it is the anger itself' (2012: 190). The auditor is thus exposed to the presence of the other's mode of being. Speech is part of a bodily expression, not a purely conceptual transmission; it is the figuration of an intentional disposition whose meaning is inseparable from gestural dimensions such as pronunciation, tone, emotion, body movements – all derivatives of the wider expressive act which condition conceptual content.

Hearing the speech of another is to encounter a certain 'style of being' – that is, a way of being in the world – and perhaps to take up this style as one's own. That is, to hear is, at least initially, to have one's own body – that is, one's own perceptual disposition – taken over by another: 'Everything happens as if the other person's intention inhabited my body, or as if my intentions inhabited his body [...] Communication is accomplished when my behaviour finds in this pathway its own pathway' (2012: 191). Rather than sharing self-contained conceptual objects, speech is a kind of body swapping, perceiving from the point of view of the other, including the other's emotional state. As Merleau-Ponty argues elsewhere: 'As an embodied subject I am exposed to the other person, just as he is to me, and I *identify* myself with the person speaking before me' (Merleau-Ponty, 1973: 18). He continues, in an image consistent with our earlier discussion of ancient rhetoric:

> Whether speaking or listening, I project myself into the other person, I introduce him into my own self. Our conversation resembles a struggle between two athletes in a tug-of-war. The speaking "I" abides in its body. Rather than imprisoning it, language is like a magic machine for transporting the "I" into the other person's perspective (1973: 19).

To communicate in this way, he argues, implies a 'depersonalised' layer of one's body that is irreducible to consciousness and that accommodates itself to the presence of the other. Of course, subsequently we may reflect on what is said or heard. But even here we are attuned to the force with which it is said, to degrees of sympathy or hostility with its hesitancy or ambivalence, for example. We may engage in debate and argument to test how firmly the emotion is connected to conceptual content. Much social and political debate is even spent *resisting* the implications of speech, policing language, taking up a distance from undertones or explicit gestures that we cannot accept. But we do this precisely because language is a way of inhabiting the world, committing us to a certain style of being, and thus speech always exceeds its strictly conceptual content.

Speech, then, can be conceived as part of what the body does more generally. It participates in making a world appear; it gives presence to its world by figuring the horizon inside which subjects are perceptually attuned. But, like the body, it does not readily appear as such itself. We do not think of the steps we take on our path as somehow 'constituting' the path; we are, instead, absorbed into the direction and purpose it offers by our walking along it. We do not always reflect on how what we say or hear constitutes our world but direct ourselves, instead, to what is talked about. Speech and language supply an 'outer skin' for bodies that are perpetually in motion, enabling us to test the contours of experience as well as, at other times, to reflect on and then critique it. The body-subject is part of a largely invisible, 'pre-personal' background out of which visible (or perceptible) things come to the fore. Yet it is from this corporeally lived experience – rather than a disembodied mind – that language, discourse and speech seek out their underlying grip on the world and help us inhabit it. As Coole underlines: 'It is in experience that discourses, ideologies, and sedimented practices are reproduced, and it is in lived experience and perceptions of dysfunctions and lacunae that resistance is first motivated and appears' (Coole, 2007a: 107).

The Flesh of the World

In later work, Merleau-Ponty began referring to the invisible or unconscious dimension of experience, out of which determinate objects come to be posited, as 'the flesh'. The flesh refers not to the material body (that is, its skin and muscle) but, more abstractly, to the 'elemental' ground of embodied existence generally; that is, the rich, obscure fabric of conscious and unconscious sensation from which the experienced world is engendered (see Merleau-Ponty, 1968: 139). With the flesh, Merleau-Ponty was signalling that the body did not merely inhabit a world but was, more fundamentally, *part of it*. He came to this view after suspecting that his earlier work had overemphasised the body's relation to conscious experience. Instead, the flesh signifies a deeper ontology of the body, the generative source from which subjectivity and objectivity are themselves constituted: 'There is', he claimed, 'a reciprocal insertion and intertwining of one in the other' (1968: 138). What characterised the flesh was partly captured in the concept of the 'chiasm' – the idea of 'crossing over', often known in the rhetorical figure of 'chiasmus'. The chiasm referred to the essential reversibility of perceiver and perceived, where to be a seer one must also be able to be seen. Another example is the way hands can both touch and be touched, as we redirect our attention from one to the other (1968: 133, 141). The flesh captures the encompassing possibilities of reversibility, the principle of a fundamental intertwining of bodies with their social and material worlds – not just in their own perceptual frame as discussed earlier but as an open set of possibilities – or Being – from which distinct ways of being emerge.

Our embodied existence, Merleau-Ponty implies, is not just a matter of being *in* but, more fundamentally, being *of* a world of contingently realised body possibilities: for example, as we employ technologies or features of the environment that extend our capacity to objectify the world and take up new ways of engaging it; or, in a more political sense, how people whose bodies are objectified find new ways of asserting their subjectivity in order to resist and alter their condition. The flesh does not describe a domain of pure contingency or 'chaos', he argued, since we are constrained to incarnate its possibilities via our bodies, with their own limitations, and not from just any perspective (1968: 146). But our bodily participation in the 'flesh of the world' (where we and the world are bound to each other) suggests a dynamic of constantly shifting and modifiable forces *beneath awareness* that provokes and stimulates our comportment. Here Merleau-Ponty resists the common criticism of phenomenology: namely, that it refers all experience to a unified and integrated subject that is taken to be centre of its world. Whether understood in terms of a cognising consciousness or as a perceiving body, this assumed centrality grants subjectivity a spurious coherence and order. Instead, his later work points to a subtle 'anti-humanist' stance that, while it explores beyond conscious perception, nonetheless remains attentive to the complexity of experience (see Coole, 2007a). The notion of the flesh implies that the body-subject – that layer of corporeal experience through which we make sense of our world – is itself embedded in a deeper communion with forces that are unknown to consciousness and that predispose it towards its environment. It alerts us to the invisible recesses and shifting layers of embodied existence beyond the self-directed subject of perception.

Merleau-Ponty's later work invites us to think of the body no longer as enclosed within a familiar and accommodating milieu but as contingently inhabiting a world that constantly opens onto unknown possibilities; bodily subjectivity is perpetually wrestling with multiple, evanescent forces that fall outside its perceptual frame. One way to think of this is in relation to the experience of pain. Bodies in pain are often distracted by a sense of being out of control, compelled to react rather than comfortably feeling their way around the environment. Pain is simultaneously 'in' us but it exists as something that is not ours. The experience of pain can be of overwhelming agony or just annoyingly niggling, an unspecifiable source of persistent discomfort and anxiety that absorbs us into our physical world and prevents us form moving freely. Either way, pain reveals the intrinsic reversibility of our body via the presence of something wholly 'other' in us that won't let go. The body in pain is neither purely subject nor object but a distressing intertwining of each.

If, for some readers of Merleau-Ponty, the flesh invokes an intimate continuity with the environment, whose abundant efficacy may positively surprise us (see, for example, Mensch, 2009), others point to a darker implication. The flesh can also be manifest as a threatening presence on the edge of our experiential horizons that disturbs our perceptual grip on the world, akin to what Lacan called 'the real' to describe the monstrous over-fullness of the world when stripped of its familiar symbolic surface (see Becker and Manoussakis, 2018; Recalcati, 2016). Indeed it might even be linked to Freud's idea of the 'uncanny' (SE XVII: 219–52): the strange, haunting sensation of something familiar yet opaque that interrupts everyday experience. The uncanny signals the re-emergence of repressed feelings, or bodily forces, that cannot be assimilated to the knowing self and which generate a diffuse feeling of unease. Likewise, the flesh may give rise to visceral sensations of alterity that in our everyday experience we refuse or avoid. For Dylan Trigg (2014), for example, Merleau-Ponty's later work reminds us that the body always consists of an 'unhuman' or alien dimension that is typically screened out of view by its everyday comportment but which returns in moments of shock or disorder. On such occasions this presence bursts forth to produce horror at the 'Thing'-like qualities of our subjective condition, the way our bodies are always caught up in forces beyond our control. For example, the agoraphobic sensation of an overbearing environment crushing the perceptual space of experience (see Trigg, 2017). Or think of the sense of disgust, guilt or shame at historical 'scars' and 'wounds' that bodies frequently bear. Such experiences – experiences that won't let go of us – suggest profound and destabilising dimensions of the flesh with which the body must constantly wrestle even as it makes a meaningful world (see Kearney, 2018).

The flesh, then, transcends experience but, in shaping the body's perceptual organisation, it reminds us that the subject is forever confronting the limits to its being, sometimes as positive extensions but also as haunting pains, vulnerabilities, threats and fears. That is to say, the lived incarnation of our world is itself generated and shaped by corporeal connections beyond intelligible experience. Here Merleau-Ponty offers his own account of what today is called the dimension of 'the political'. This refers to the underlying contingency and openness of the boundaries of social existence and human identity. The political describes the condition of ontological indeterminacy that prevents any final closure or foundation to existence (see Marchart, 2007). What is unique to Merleau-Ponty's philosophy and especially his idea of the flesh, is that this fundamental openness – and the turbulence it manifests – is conceived primarily as a quality of the body (see Mazzocchi, 2013). This insight, I want to suggest next, points us to a 'carnal politics' to speech and rhetoric that will inform the rest of this book.

A Carnal Politics of Rhetoric

Merleau-Ponty's philosophy tells us that subjectivity is irreducible to conscious awareness and encompasses the body as a whole. This subject is not isolated from its world, enclosed in the mind, but is always intertwined with the material and spatial environment through which it moves. It is complex, layered, and attuned to the multiple textures of its perception, sometimes to the point that its subjectivity is not fully its own at all. Speech and language, then, are better understood as modes of inhabiting this shifting world than as mere messages about what goes on in it. Speech incarnates a world, it directs our intentionality and folds us into sensations and orientations that bring us into proximity with the flesh of our existence – the way our perceptual attentions are rooted in contingent bodily relations that may be styled otherwise. These insights point us to the corporeal qualities of human discourse in at least two, related, respects. The idea of the body-subject alerts us to the way sense is so often enacted *in bodily terms*. The flesh, however, signals the hidden underside of this bodily sense, the invisible stuff of existence out of which perception itself arises. Let me sketch how these might be thought in rhetorical terms.

The role of the lived body in communicative practices is now a well established topic in academic literature, much of which draws upon Merleau-Ponty's work (see, for example, Grosz, 1994). The body is where power is 'inscribed', where discourses are given material form, for instance in medical practices, or claims to gender identity and their subversion. Merleau-Ponty is perhaps distinctive in that he underlines the motility of the body, rather than its being a passive material pushed into shape by external forces. The body-subject highlights what the body itself does, how it *makes* meaning through its tactility, its gestures and the schemata that map the spaces in which it moves. The body implicitly understands its own possibilities and limits; our ability to make inferences and to affirm the normative validity (or not) of ideas is a correlate of this bodily understanding. Things often need to 'feel' right if we are to accept them as right.

This notion of a body correlate is perhaps most well known in the work of Lakoff and Johnson on conceptual metaphor (see Lakoff and Johnson, 1980; 1999). In their view, the body functions as the perceptual bedrock of conceptual thought. This is clear, for example, in the way metaphors of orientation support much of our cognitive reasoning, enabling an unreflective receptivity that is figured through body or body-related schemata. Basically, we understand speech only because our conceptual frameworks derive from fundamental orientational capacities we tacitly presuppose. The architecture of thought and discourse is organised, they argue, through implicit (but often explicit) reference to bodies in space: we describe conditions as if they were physical containers ('I'm "in" love') or we present arguments as if they were journeys (where we 'set out' to eventually 'arrive' at a certain point), and so on. This idea of conceptual metaphor has been extended to rhetorical types of analysis by Lakoff and others to explore how specific moral and political arguments repeatedly make sense by analogies to bodily states (see Lakoff, 2002; Musolff, 2004).

But Lakoff and Johnson are concerned primarily with conceptual content, the stuff of cognition by which we think and reason. Less attention, however, is given to actual bodies and the way that individuals and groups themselves also instantiate embodied argumentative stances. The body politics of national leaders – Russian President Vladimir Putin's bare back horse riding or his judo practice, for example – are a notable part of how authority is symbolically projected through bodily choreography. In a different way, crowds and mobilised groups generate a corporeal density that is hard to ignore and generates its own, sometimes threatening, atmospheres (see Davies, 2018: 3–8). Bodies bared, self-immolating, blocking, and so on: even without speech bodies themselves may function as argumentative devices or props.

Merleau-Ponty's notion of the flesh, however, urges us to go beyond the visibility of the body in rhetoric to something otherwise imperceptible: namely, to forces *beneath* the surface that shape the space of bodily gesture and orientation (see Coole, 2007b). Rhetoric cannot directly represent the flesh, only draw attention to its traces, such as forms of suffering that signal the body's immersion in a deeper, often traumatic communion with the world. Because the flesh frames our body's perpetual awareness, we cannot directly perceive how we emerge from it but can only register it as a disturbing sense of contingency over the place from which we speak or are spoken to. The flesh is often encountered indirectly as a 'stain' or a cut that disrupts the smoothness of our discourse. Rhetorically, this is not a positive conceptual gesture or expression but the presence of a discursive blockage or disruption that draws our attention to the corporeality of subjectivity.

Now, much political discourse is aimed precisely at *not* addressing the corporeal preconditions of speech. Formal public talk is attuned, rather selectively, to the very immediate objects within settled horizons and so typically withdraws attention from its own corporeality. Instead, we find this 'fleshy' dimension manifest in disruptive types of rhetoric, particularly those that address catastrophic experiences that defy assumptions of autonomous, self-determining agency. We find it in some religious discourse but also in 'confessional' rhetoric where emotions are salient. In these different forms, rhetoric brings to the fore the very corporeality of human speech by exposing its hidden flesh. These raw, frequently painful discourses draw us towards the carnality of experience that lies outside our normal attention. The carnal politics of rhetoric refers us to the ways public speech and language intermittently succeed in getting beneath the skin of experience to register hitherto ignored or unexplored recesses and wells of experience. At such moments, established modes of perception, reasoning, and speaking, along with associated sediments of accepted taste and feeling, are stripped of their assumed integrity and familiarity. It is in these moments – such as the arrival of the #METOO movement or the recent explosion of populisms of various orientations – that new, different and sometimes disconcerting possibilities for inhabiting the world come into view.

Conclusion

The subject of speech, I have argued, should be conceived not as an isolated mind but as an embodied entity that is inseparable from the world it inhabits. More than merely expressing opinions, speech and argument are ways to coordinate and manoeuvre subjects, often regardless of what they may actually think. Ancient rhetoricians were attentive to this implicit corporeality but modern thought has rather neglected it. With phenomenologists such as Merleau-Ponty, however, we have a way of bringing it back into consideration. His work invites us to see how rhetoric lodges subjects in the spaces and routines that make up their shared phenomenal worlds. It permits them to negotiate obstacles, to confront new experiences and to figure ways of being that maintain some degree of coherence. But the embodied subject of experience is rooted in a fleshy corporeality that extends beyond perceptual awareness and disposes it unconsciously towards its world in ways it cannot always master or fathom. At times, however, rhetoric can expose elements of this flesh and, when it does so, we are summoned to feel and talk very differently.

My aim in this chapter has been to initiate a way of thinking about speech and rhetoric that displaces the tendency to reduce it all to conceptual thought. Although I set aside exploration of Merleau-Ponty's work from now on, his insights concerning bodily subjectivity, language as inhabiting a world, and the idea of the flesh as an experience of alterity, all figure centrally in my discussion of psychoanalysis, a discipline that he himself described as a 'philosophy of the flesh'. I shall argue in the remainder of this book that psychoanalytic thought allows us to understand better the embodied dynamics of speech by foregrounding the movement of desire.

2. Voicing Desire

In this chapter I begin to make the case for conceiving public speech as a medium for inciting and coordinating desire. To do so I draw on psychoanalysis, a tradition of thought uniquely attentive to how bodily feelings are implicated in everyday judgements and choices, especially regarding our attachments and aversions, and in stories we tell ourselves and others to make our behaviour seem consistent and unforced. More than that, psychoanalysis tells us that the mind is not a wholly unified or independent agency but is inseparable from unconscious organic impulses and energies that impress themselves upon its perceptions and attitudes. In that respect, psychoanalysis is a 'philosophy of the flesh', as Merleau-Ponty claimed; it understands mental activity as entangled with embodied forces that excite us but also threaten our sense of coherence. It reminds us that often we are inclined to hide ourselves from the truth of our motivations because they are unacceptable or do not fit with our self-image. When we connect that insight to rhetoric (as I begin to do in this chapter and continue in the next) we start to understand how public speech and argument involve strategies to repel, contain or sustain our desires. Like the ancient understanding of rhetoric, mentioned in the last chapter, psychoanalysis permits us to grasp how rhetorical speech helps make public sense by shifting weight and directing force.

In setting out these claims, I make reference primarily to the work of Jacques Lacan. This is so for a number of reasons. First, Lacan's ideas make central what is more or less implied in all psychoanalytic thought: namely, the divided and precarious condition of subjectivity. True mental illness, surmises one Lacanian commentator, consists in the illusion that one is a coherent self at all (Recalcati, 2012a: 29). The subject for Lacan is constitutively 'split' and experiences its desire only through forms of incompleteness – such as loss, division, or dissatisfaction. Second, Lacan was especially interested in human discourse, not as a practical tool to share messages but as a means to manage and disguise the subject's ontological division. Discourse is a medium of desire, not only because it expresses our demands but, also, because it displaces the discomforts of our incompleteness. As Lundberg puts, for Lacan the 'failed unicity' of the subject compels it to seek 'feigned unicity' in discourse (Lundberg, 2012: 2–3). Third, and finally, Lacan provides a framework to understand how the dynamics of discourse are never located entirely in a subjective interior – conceived as individuated containers of minds – but, rather, in its wider relationships, particularly with the enigmatic 'Other' to which it is closely bound. Eccentric to ourselves, we never 'own' our own speech nor speak 'authentically' as individuals. Voicing desire is always done by way of the Other. This initial framework, I suggest, will be vital in thinking critically about rhetoric and rhetorical analysis.

In this chapter I set out the initial grounds for thinking about subjectivity and speech by way of psychoanalytical theory, and through Lacan's ideas in particular. In the chapter that follows, I explore more closely the relevance of these arguments to rhetoric. Before considering Lacan's contribution, however, let me first discuss Freud and psychoanalysis generally.

Plausible Stories

We frequently think of public speaking in rather instrumental terms, that is, as a way of getting others to think what we want or, at very least, stopping them thinking things we don't want. Persuasion, we are invited to believe, is a type of artful deception or manipulation whereby tried and tested techniques are applied to our discourse and – ta da! – audiences laugh at our jokes, tremble at the sad stories and, by the end, feel the passionate honesty of the message. This is not a wholly inaccurate way to describe how many go about preparing for public speech and, for that reason, there are numerous texts that instruct on how to apply techniques to our discourse so that we can 'communicate with success'. At the root of these approaches is, commonly, a more or less elaborated psychology of emotions that explains how different audience responses are triggered by deploying certain metaphors, narrative styles, or presentational techniques (see, for example, Cialdini, 2007). More recently, psychological insights have been offered by developments in neuroscience, which identify specific causal processes for emotional activity in the brain and instruct readers on how such knowledge can be utilised as tools of communication, for instance in 'nudging' the ranking of our preferences or 'framing' our perception of moral issues (see Thaler and Sunstein, 2009; Lakoff, 2002).

Psychoanalysis, however, offers a different view of how emotions and feelings work. Which is to say, it has a quite distinct view of human subjectivity (see Frosh, 1989; Parker, 2015). By consequence, its approach to speech and language is also different. Whereas for psychology, mental behaviour is typically separated into discrete 'modules', or functional processes, which are modelled and explained scientifically, psychoanalysis regards the person as a whole (if a somewhat discordant one) whose different mental functions overlap, mutually influence each other, and constantly interact with social relations. In cognitive psychology, for instance, speech is a more or less transparent reflection of rule-governed processes (Frosh, 1989: 131). But, for psychoanalysis, a person's own sense of selfhood is vital to how their various functions operate; how they narrate their experiences – the story they tell about themselves or the things and people that matter to them or bring them anxiety – is vital to how they actually behave.

For psychoanalysis, then, language embodies and sustains (as well as constrains) meaning rather than exhibits rules of thought. Where psychology is concerned with the 'syntax' of the cognitive systems it describes, psychoanalysis is preoccupied with the 'semantics' (that is, the meanings) that motivate and integrate subjective intentions (Frosh,

1989: 14–15, 134–42). Psychoanalytic therapy is known as the 'talking cure' precisely because exploring meaning is considered vital to understanding emotional disorder and eventually overcoming it. Both approaches look to unconscious subjective processes to explain how people act: for psychology these are typically functional routines that can be described and ascribed 'universal' status. But, for psychoanalysis, they are more deeply rooted configurations of meaning and feeling, which may be regular but also highly particular, mostly repressed and hence accessible largely through accidental disclosures or aberrant behaviours that usually make no sense to the individuals concerned.

Since its inception with Sigmund Freud, psychoanalysis has been interested in the ways we refuse to engage or even acknowledge certain parts of our self. Often these parts feel distressing, confused, angry or even obscene. For Freud, they are remnants of unconscious wishes refused full access to awareness. Although, on occasion, such wishes may inexplicably come to the surface and interrupt our habits, we quickly dismiss them or shake them off. Freud's whole enterprise involved not merely identifying underlying emotional disorders but, moreover, drawing attention to the habit of unconscious 'censorship' or even conscious 'resistance' when they are otherwise transparent (SE22: 15). People regularly construct what Adam Phillips describes as 'plausible stories' to account for their conduct, filtering out or minimising what disturbs or doesn't make sense, so as to sustain a narrative that fits with their preferred view of themselves or their world (Phillips, 2014: 9). That way, it is possible to 'inhabit a world', as Merleau-Ponty puts it, with some degree of coherence. These stories are plausible in so far as they appear consistent with what we or others expect to hear or prefer to know. All sorts of outlandish or excessive feelings and experiences are thereby explained away. The stories we tell, the principles and values we defend, the arguments we insist upon winning – these can all be ways of managing and, often, disguising tensions we would rather not, or simply cannot, admit to.

Psychoanalysis starts, then, with this view of language as a medium for mediating unconscious bodily impulses and the social or public expectations of individuals. It is, to echo the discussion in the previous chapter, a means to negotiate the 'flesh' of bodily energies that provoke us to desire. Speech is crucial because we cannot detect these desires without also listening to how they are filtered and selected to become plausible. Much of Freud's published work – from the *Interpretation of Dreams*, to his analysis of jokes and his case studies of patient therapy – involved developing ways to critically read people's words and behaviour this way. Speech is not therefore a transparent window on the unconscious but, rather, a medium that itself resists and distorts desires. This is something we learn to do from childhood and so, later in life, our words disguise the compromises demanded of us as children for entry into the world of adults. As Phillips (2014: 42) puts it: 'language keeps referring us back [...] to the first uneasy rendezvous between our bodies and the language they were compelled to use'. The psychoanalyst therefore has to interpret what she hears, to discriminate the recurrent evasions, resistances and knots in thinking that suggest an ongoing struggle with what now lies outside of conscious awareness.

Freud was particularly interested in language and the way it simultaneously reveals and obscures unconscious forces. The interpretive task of the psychoanalyst was to understand this complex symbolic work. Referring to dreams, slips of the tongue, jokes or otherwise discarded remarks and observations, his thesis was that language was the primary site of unresolved conflicts between what individuals desire and what or how they *should* speak. Language – in the broad sense, including speech but other forms of symbolic activity – is a medium to forge 'compromises' between movements of 'psychical energy' that cannot be reconciled and which, periodically, struggle for pre-eminence (SE22: 16). People unconsciously select words, symbols and styles to give form to their wishes but also to keep them under control and to hold back what threatens them. Psychoanalytic interpretation involves reading these words and symbols as the movement of metaphorical surfaces that 'condense' and 'displace' bodily urges to satisfy forbidden or feared wishes. The psychoanalyst has to listen not as an ordinary interlocutor concerned with the 'manifest' content of the patient's thoughts but, rather, as an interpreter of 'latent' meanings found in the patient's hesitations, word errors, or repeated phrases where something other tries to speak.

But what are these wishes and how are they in conflict? Freud famously argues that the psyche is organised around the management of its 'drives' – organic and primarily sexual impulses whose excitations stimulate the human organism. The force of the drives are translated into mental representations that motivate the individual to find satisfaction in certain objects (see SE14: 117–40). In his early explorations, Freud understood the process of drive satisfaction as being akin to the transference of energy: drives comprise stimulations by organic energy in the body, often around highly sensitive erogenous zones, which creates tensions that cause psychical discomfort and are 'discharged' by creating neural 'paths' to actual or imagined objects, thus giving pleasure to the individual in the form of relief (see SE1: 312–22).

The drives are thus neither purely organic nor mental but something 'on the frontier between the mental and the somatic' (SE14: 122), moving quantities of physical energy that transform into symbolic constructs. As such, they are, he admits, highly mobile. Drive energy is channelled into multiple forms, finding discharge by way of various paths depending on what society holds to be acceptable. That way, managing drive satisfaction – through what Freud called the 'pleasure principle': the effort to minimise the stress of excessive excitation by selective discharge – aligns desire with the demands of sheer survival and social cooperation. The mechanisms of the psyche – and in particular, the 'ego' – function to coordinate the drives or inhibit them altogether. In Freud's early view, psychic activity was described as a 'hydraulic' system that brings the energies of the organism into a stable 'equilibrium'; the ego was thus a means to harmonise drive impulses with the pragmatic demands of reality. By displacing drives onto alternative paths, or repressing them, however, the overall system is perpetually held in tension. This can lead to psychic discomfort and neurotic 'symptoms' as the drive seeks alternative paths to discharge, via circuitous routes such as in dreams or 'accidental' behaviours. Neuroses, such as hysteria, were described by Freud as 'a substitute for what did not happen' because the drive was blocked, finding release instead by way of symptoms that bring degrees of relief and distress (SE16: 294). From phantom pains to obsessive attachments, bouts of paranoia or inexplicable fear, the body manifests aberrant behaviours that indicate unresolved internal conflicts.

This brief sketch presents Freud's account of the psyche in rather naturalistic terms. It is certainly true that Freud saw his work as a contribution to 'scientific' (and especially natural-scientific) knowledge. But psychoanalysis is also an 'interpretive' mode of enquiry because its focus is less on objective causes and more on subjective processes and their social and emotional consequences. The individual is never an isolated organism but always a person socialised into accepted ways of managing and fulfilling its wishes in order to uphold communal expectations. Born unable to look after itself, the human infant is wholly dependent on its carers, family and community for both its education and survival. The management and organisation of its drives and the practical demands of reality are therefore given primacy over direct drive satisfaction through intimate and lengthy socialisation.

The structural organisation of the unconscious is famously understood by Freud, in general terms, as the formation of psychic agencies that enable the partial satisfaction of drive impulses and ensure the inhibition of others. Freud's concepts of the 'id', 'ego', and 'superego' – or the unknowable unconscious, the partially aware organising self, and the commands of social authority – comprise the key agencies in this structure. But the development of the psyche through different phases is also fundamental, as his discussion of the 'Oedipus Complex' – 'the nucleus of the neuroses' – highlights (SE16: 330–38). The gradual establishment of a governing ego that inhibits the libidinal demands of the id and aligns them with those of the social superego is achieved only at a tremendous emotional cost: the repression of desires for the mother, the identification with a feared father, and a lifetime spent repeating this lost attachment alongside an urge to find more fulfilling satisfaction. Freud's later explorations of society and politics centre precisely on the attachments, aversions, idealisations and hostilities that are rooted in the painful traumas of individual's early familial socialisation (see SE21: 57–145; Brunner, 2001).

Freud sometimes presented a tragic picture of the individual as an emotionally damaged soul forever replaying the traumas of childhood. But even if we do not accept this bleak picture, we can still grasp what his account of psychic life entails. Above all, the individual is irreducible to its own self-perceptions. Self-awareness and cognitive activity are only a part of psychic organisation. Much of what motivates us and provokes us to feel lies outside of consciousness and is utterly inaccessible to direct knowledge. Moreover, this unconscious is dynamic, rather than inert: it actively orients us towards certain objects and away from others. Psychoanalysis emerged at a time when the human organism was increasingly regarded by medical science as a system perpetually on the verge of catastrophic crisis, or 'disequilibrium' (see Geroulanos and Meyers, 2018). In Freud's account, unconscious energy is persistently brimming up to consciousness, disrupting its smooth functioning, and messing with its choices as it negotiates desires and social expectations. Our conscious experiences are often strangely saturated with memories and sensations we did not invite; we are plagued by anxieties and aversions we cannot understand; and often we sabotage our own achievements and successes for no good reason. Indeed, the point here is that conscious reason is not the centrepiece of psychic life at all. It would be easy to say that some kind of blind impulse is at work. But, in fact, it is something less coherent: a strange amalgam of structured but unwilled wishes and laboured rationalisations often dominate our psychic experience. The plausible stories that circulate in human experience are rooted not in a single, decisive factor but in the constant, groping effort to make sense of the uncanniness of experience by rendering it consistent, smoothing over what seems perverse.

Psychoanalysis, then, offers a unique framework for understanding the bodily grip of the stories on which we frequently rely to rationalise the perplexing contradictions of personal and social life.

Freud supplies coordinates for a theory of persuasion focused on how symbols mediate the balancing of our 'inner' and 'outer' worlds. Unlike psychological thinking, upon which speech writers and instructors rely, psychoanalysis regards speech (and other forms of cultural production) as a medium to stabilise conflictual psychic processes (see Minsky, 1998). Freud offers an account of subjectivity characterised not by cognitive rules and instrumental routines but, rather, by the constantly shifting forces of the flesh: tensions and torsions with which individuals perpetually struggle to find poise in the stream of their emotional lives. In this, he returns us, in part, to the idea of rhetoric raised in the last chapter: namely, a practice that follows a logic of embodiment rather than one of pure conceptuality. To give more precision to this view, however, I now turn to the radical insights brought to psychoanalytic theory by Jacques Lacan.

The Lacanian Subject

Lacan's work is not an obvious source for thinking about public speech or rhetoric. Lacan is a notoriously obscure writer; his ideas are frequently opaque and his style of teaching, which employs algebraic notion, sometimes wilfully abstruse. Malcolm Bowie even suggests that, in his major writings, 'Lacan cultivates obscurity' (Bowie, 1991: 12). This is partly because he doesn't want his ideas reduced to easily digestible nuggets. The unconscious – whose workings he tries to convey in his own mode of communicating – is too complex to be neatly summed up. Nonetheless Lacan is profoundly interested in speech and language, regarding them as central to the whole enterprise of psychoanalysis: the unconscious, he claims, is 'structured like language'. Lacan is, by consequence, particularly drawn to rhetoric (see Lundberg, 2012).

Before considering what rhetorical analysis might gain from Lacan's writings, I want to sketch his view of the subject. Building on Freud's work, Lacan conceives the subject as irretrievably split: 'the unconscious is always manifested as that which vacillates in a split in the subject' (Lacan, 1977: 28). The abundant forces of the unconscious exceed the symbolic forms through which the subject articulates itself. It therefore experiences itself in various ways as incomplete. But this intrinsic 'lack' (1977: 26) is precisely what compels it towards objects of desire – people and ideas, as well as empirical objects – that promise it satisfaction by closing the gap. Of course, these objects never fully satisfy it and the subject regularly seeks out new targets for desire. In Lacan's theory, like Freud's, simply being a stable, functioning individual is therefore something of a struggle. For the subject never fully coincides with a unitary and complete account of its 'self': its unconscious overflows the given shapes of selfhood, or identity, and 'something other demands to be realized' (1977: 25). A therapeutic cure can therefore never be one that restores the subject to a 'natural' balance. Lacan was especially critical of (usually American) psychoanalysts who sought to affirm the individual's ego as the inner core of stable and 'autonomous' selfhood that might be brought back into conformity with societal demands (2006: 346): 'It is autonomous! That's a good one!' (2006: 350). To take the unconscious seriously was to accept that the subject would never master its desires but was, instead, constituted *through* them and thus never in harmony with itself. Psychoanalytic therapy could only ever bring patients to understand and recognise this situation, not overcome it: 'The goal is not, as people believe, to adapt to a more or less well-defined or well-organised reality [*réel*], but to get one's own reality – that is, one's own desire – recognized' (Lacan, 2013: 37).

Lacan frequently describes his approach to the subject in terms of three different 'registers' known as the imaginary, the symbolic, and the real (see Lacan, 2013: 3–52). The imaginary register is that of images by means of which the subject identifies itself as an autonomous and unified ego. The symbolic denotes the register of language, knowledge, and all the structured systems through which individuals enter into intersubjective (or social) relations. The real, by contrast, is the domain of unformed energies excluded by the other two registers. The real refers to the organic, bodily impulses and urges that are largely unassimilable to images or to the necessarily selective structures of language. Together the three registers organise the totality of the subject's perceptual and emotional disposition. Let us explore each in turn.

Each register has a part to play in organising the way the subject desires: the imaginary supplies an image, or composite picture, of the ego as a coherent and integrated unity. In his early theory of the 'mirror stage', Lacan argues that an infant makes a qualitative leap in its early development after jubilantly identifying with its reflection in the mirror (usually assisted by the directions and gaze of its carer) (see 2006: 75–81). The mirror image supplies a contoured picture that fascinates the subject, who assumes it as a true reflection of its self: grasped as something whole, homogenous, unified in its body and autonomous from those who care for it. 'Fascination is absolutely essential to the phenomenon of the constitution of the ego. The uncoordinated, incoherent diversity of the primitive fragmentation gains its unity in so far as it is fascinated' (Lacan, 1988: 50). But the fascinating image of a 'pre-established harmony' is illusory. The infant is not in charge of its still fragmented limbs and bodily functions, it remains dependent for its basic needs and development on others, and thus its autonomy is considerably limited. But the image is a first step in the formation – or what Lacan describes as 'misrecognition' – of itself as a desiring entity. Thereafter, the child organises its physical needs and demands in terms of this permanently anticipated image of autonomy and integrity. Assuming itself as a separate, integrated ego it then learns to perceive the wider world in terms of other discrete objects that are separate from it and available, or not, to its desires.

But this is a paradoxical and unstable experience of perceptual and bodily autonomy. Formed through identification with an image, the ego is always reliant on the assurance of an externally given source – as Lacan says, the 'ego really is an object' onto which we invest our unconscious desires, not a natural or pre-given feature (Lacan, 1988: 49). The child depends on this 'other' image that it mistakes as a representation, leading it then to confuse itself with the numerous images with which it identifies (other children, for example). Moreover, the imaginary register is profoundly asymmetric and hence unstable. It is fundamentally bipolar in form, imposing a simple and static logic of 'inside' or 'outside' (see Recalcati, 2012b: 37–44). The infant experiences the world starkly in terms of things that are assimilable to its wishes and things that are not. The latter are often perceived as a crushing threat to its unity and autonomy.

The imaginary register offers a fragile assumption of internal sovereignty but at the price of an underlying tendency to narcissism, alienation and paranoia. Unable to judge when another person is assimilable to its desires, the early subject is prone to intense feelings of dispossession, envy, and to aggressiveness (Lacan, 2006: 82–101). Although in later life it depends less and less on its imaginary ego for a sense of identity, a self-image remains integral to the organisation of its experience and is often a source of resistance in therapy. Alienation and paranoia – that is, feelings of inner discordance and reliance upon an identity that is never entirely one's own, and anxiety at the intrusions of others into one's assumed autonomy – remain common experiences for many adults. All individuals are fascinated by images and ideas that figure them as idealised unities, unique masters of themselves, and especially attractive to others. The imaginary nourishes this unconscious assumption of bodily integrity that promises a coherent relation to the world but also makes us vulnerable to our encounters there (see Nasio, 2013). It is precisely the unsteady grip of adopted images – and not a genuine intrusion from outside – that gives rise to paranoid feelings. Lacan's early investigations thus explored the idea that psychotic disorders stemmed from narcissistic delusions whereby subjects confused their own self-image with that of others, sometimes leading to forms of violent and hostile behaviour (see Lacan, 2006: 95–8, 356; Vanheule, 2014: 9–30).

The symbolic register, by contrast, involves access by the subject to a more complex network of interrelated roles and identities than is permitted by the imaginary. Although language is fully acquired at a later developmental stage, in fact the infant is always immersed in the speech of its parents and carers. In accordance with the structural linguistics of Ferdinand de Saussure, whose work was highly influential in the 1950s and 60s in France, Lacan understood language as a shifting system of symbolic differences rather than fixed references to objects (see Lacan, 2006: 412–41). At their most basic level, linguistic 'signs' consist of 'signifiers' (for example, words) and 'signifieds' (the concepts or things to which signifiers refer). Signifiers acquire their value by phonetic and conceptual differences within a wider system of associations and relations, not by anything positive independent of them. Speech therefore involves assembling 'chains' of signifiers from this wider system, invoking differences that are not spoken (just as identifying a 'hat' implies – but does not actually declare – a phonetic difference from 'cat' or a conceptual difference from 'scarf'). Lacan's major innovation consists for many in his effort to bring psychoanalytical thought and practice to a better grasp of speech and language as the central medium of psychical organisation (see Lacan, 2006: 197–268; Lang, 1986).

Symbolic exchange involves the invocation of both presences and absences: first, by deploying signifiers that re-present things that are not directly present and, second, via a system of unacknowledged differences that give signifiers meaning. For Lacan, it is the movement of presence and absence by the signifier, not its alignment with the signified as such, that has primacy in psychic life. Indeed, it is the dynamic 'sliding' of signifiers that makes speech so revealing of subjectivity and that links psychoanalytic interpretation to the figures of rhetoric (Lacan, 2006: 221–22). When Lacan says that 'the unconscious is structured like a language' (1977: 20), he is partly suggesting that we internalise these systems of interconnecting signifiers so profoundly that our whole relationship to the world is utterly inconceivable without them. Our most intimate perceptions, desires and feelings take the form of myriad, mobile symbolic associations and differences, which express and constrain how we experience unconscious desires. For example, language frequently carries the weight of intense feelings, either directly or by association, and cannot always easily be spoken. 'Words', he underlines, 'are caught up in all the body images that captivate the subject' (2006: 248). They have materiality that exerts a profound force upon us. Indeed, the subject, Lacan suggests, should be 'defined as the effect of the signifier' in so far as signifiers capture or 'petrify' it (1977: 207). Moreover, the symptom of emotional disorder is also 'structured like a language' as disruptions, fixations or even absences in signification are the medium through which the unconscious struggles to speak (2006: 223).

For Lacan, the subject enters into the world of symbolic differences not only by acquiring speech but also by accommodating the roles and functions in its family and, later, other social systems. In that respect, the symbolic domain encompasses not only verbal structures but all patterns of social organisation. Collectively, these systems constitute a whole 'symbolic order' that overwrites the subject's imaginary identity and coordinates it by relating it to others. The great advantage of the symbolic order is the release of tension it offers, enabling the subject to 'transcend the fundamental aggressive relation' entailed in imaginary identification (Lacan, 2013: 25). No longer focussed exclusively on its narcissistic ego, the subject absorbs ever wider and more complex meanings and thereby learns to place itself in flexible, manageable relations with other subjects. The symbolic register therefore 'decentres' the subject, enabling it to take up a variety of differentially positioned roles in relation to numerous, co-existing identities: as daughter, sister, citizen, engineer, and so on. These distinct significations, which articulate and recombine infinitely, disperse personal identity across a range of differences rather than concentrate them in one alone; their relational nature enables fluid combinations and differentiations.

However, the capacity to speak and interact socially also comes at a cost. Lacan's understanding of the transition from predominantly imaginary to symbolic registration reworks Freud's account of the Oedipus Complex (see Recalcati, 2012b: 99–100). Successfully acquiring language and entering symbolic relations is, for Lacan, a traumatic process correlative with forging one's sexual identity. Entrance into the symbolic order involves relinquishing an intense imaginary (and so bodily experienced) bond with the mother (or carer) and identifying, instead, with a place in a symbolic hierarchy. What Freud had described as a process of taking up a sexual identity is conceived by Lacan as reorganising one's desires around the punishing demands of a symbolic order. This shift is traumatic and shapes the subject's management of its desires permanently. To take up its 'symbolic mandate' (as daughter or son in the family, for example) the child relinquishes what is felt to be a profound sense of imaginary unity for the division organised around the prohibitive authority of the father. The father appears to possess some quality of attraction – the 'phallus' – that the mother desires and so the child is initially drawn to possess or be this, too. The paternal figure instantiates an order of prohibitions on desire (for example, refusing incestuous relations with the mother). Satisfying desire must now be mediated through accepted social rules, or what Lacan calls 'the Law', administered at first in the 'Name-of-the-Father' (the prohibitive paternal 'no') and later through social rules generally. To be an independent subject thus comes with the terrible burden of guilt because now one judges oneself constantly by an external standard (2013: 28–9). Although the loss of imaginary unity entailed by this symbolic order is (like all imaginary forms) fundamentally illusory, repeated submission to the symbolic Law (at home, in school, at work, and so on) will often feel like the deprivation of a comforting sense of corporeal bliss. Lacan refers to this process as 'castration' since submitting to it involves cutting away a deeply felt physical bond (Lacan, 2006: 229–31).

Hereafter, the subject learns to desire predominantly by way of symbolic systems. Its unconscious organisation comes to be structured through networks of signifiers whose potential for manipulation then creates inventive possibilities for naming desires. We express and measure our wishes by signifiers that link us to other signifiers and, thereby, to other subjects. We are thus constrained to identify and to speak in systems of meaning that precede us and order our subjectivity according to hierarchies and prohibitions that Lacan refers to as the 'Other' (with a capital o): an assumed 'locus' of authority, or truth, in the symbolic systems (of language, social relations, and so on) upon which we depend, rather than the person who speaks from that locus (Lacan, 2006: 358). The symbolic register thus necessitates 'the constitution of the subject in the field of the Other' (1977: 208). Whenever we speak, whatever we speak about, we invoke a hidden 'pact' with this authority merely by using words (2006: 358). 'Which basically means that we are always asking the Other what he desires' (2008: 38). For example, my desire to see myself as a satisfactory worker comes by 'acting professionally' in the eyes of my co-workers or managers and by meeting certain stipulated symbolic targets. We come to desire in a way that is different from the imaginary – which makes objects exclusively its own – that is, by desiring things that are symbolically connected to other signifiers accorded value.

But whose desires are these? Because desire – the insistent urge to achieve satisfaction – is now organised through an intersubjective system that operates over us, are our wishes ever genuinely our own? Or are they ways to satisfy the Other? Can we even have our own desires if they are symbolically mediated? Man's desire, claims Lacan, 'is the desire of the Other' (1977: 38). That is, what we take as our own object of desire is inextricably bound up with achieving recognition from the Other – instantiated by God, our parents, or society in general. Often, we come to moments of self-realisation when we grasp that what we have aspired to be, do or have is inherited from family or society. Indeed, this feeling often comes after we realise that achievement or acquisition of given objects of desire never really satisfy us anyway. In part that is because the symbolic organisation of desire rarely gets us direct satisfaction since it remains wholly symbolic – the marker of an absence.

So, for all the obvious and immense benefits that the symbolic register brings in terms of communication and a structured, meaningful world, it also produces disappointment, confusion and alienation. Language for Lacan is not really a tool for communication but a complex web of interconnections through which subjects submit themselves to desiring through the Other. All our conversations imply or name this assumed locus from which we seek affirmation, thereby also revealing our own dependence on something other to make our world coherent. Without language we could not desire effectively; nonetheless, with it, we all too easily feel the disappointment of our desires and the underlying sense of loss we bear simply to express them. Lacan came to see the failure to undergo symbolic castration – that is, to relinquish imaginary fullness and to learn to desire by ceding to the authority of the paternal figure – as another cause of psychosis (see Vanheule, 2014: 33–122). Without a symbolic mandate, subjects cannot adequately anchor their energies to signifiers and hold off the urge to enjoy full, unmediated satisfaction.

Finally, the register of the real refers not to 'reality' (which is a symbolic construct) but to organic impulses and energies that are expelled in the formation of the imaginary and symbolic registers. In foregrounding a set of images and in symbolically framing our social world, a vast amount of what is available to desire is filtered out. From toilet-training to managing our anger or libidinal impulses, psychic development is organised through the enforced exclusion from the body of all sorts of 'unacceptable' objects and experiences. The continued presence of these exclusions at the margins of subjectivity are described by Lacan as the real. Having no intelligible form, the real denotes not merely things we don't like or find repulsive, since those can be visualised and conceptualised. Rather, it refers to traces of something intolerable *in* such things, something 'impossible' that cannot be aligned with the pleasure principle (1977: 167). This abjection is manifest, for example, in our commonly horrified reaction to blood, viscera or faeces. It describes the unknowable and threatening edge to our meaningful world, the precarious boundary of perceptual sense and non-sense that is itself 'inaccessible' to direct experience and which, when encountered, provokes anxiety (2013: 80).

Lacan's reference to the real – which, I noted earlier, corresponds in key respects to Merleau-Ponty's concept of the flesh – implies that the subject is never fully absorbed by imaginary or symbolic registers. Indeed, the tendency to paranoia of the imaginary and the frequent inadequacy of symbolic structures to contain unconscious experience generate a constant psychic precariousness. What cannot be assimilated to the ego or rationally explained away frequently returns in the monstrous formlessness of the real – for instance in experiences that defy established norms or expectations and invoke in us a sense of utter dread. The real describes a repetitive impulse of drive energy that seeps into the dependable order and regularity of the perceived world, typically felt as uncanny, malevolent forces that threaten bodily fragmentation and unreason (Lacan, 1977: 49). Although we imagine such fears as disrupting our world from the outside – it is frequently represented as the shapeless monster of horror stories and movies – it appears not as an object but as a distortion of all sense. The real is thus part of our own psychic constitution, that fragment of unconscious desire that is repressed by the ego; its return may be activated by something external, but its force resides in the way it dissolves perceptual certainty, especially our sense of being autonomous agents in a meaningful world that we can understand and manipulate. The real is therefore not an object but rather a force of dissolution, where the boundaries that regulate desire fall apart.

Desire Beyond Pleasure

We can see how Lacan's three registers – each of which he emphasised at different stages of his career – produce an account of the individual subject as the bearer of a precarious and divided identity. The Lacanian subject is not the fully formed, self-aware, and emotionally secure individual of liberal reason but, rather, an agent that comes into being by misperceiving itself as an autonomous unity, attaches itself to rules it observes obsessively, and stands perpetually on the cusp of existential anxiety. Alienation is here not a misfortune to be overcome but, rather, constitutive of the subject as such. Yet it is precisely the disorderly and incomplete nature of the subject that generates the dynamic of its desire. The absence of intrinsic harmony around a positive foundation compels the subject perpetually to reorganise its desires so as to evade the threatening horror of the real. Rather than motivated by 'natural' instincts (for survival, say) or uniquely endowed abilities to reason (so as to produce knowledge) that help it return to a harmony with its world, the Lacanian subject is always eccentric to itself. It is, in some respects, a strangely inhuman creature since neither instinct nor reason are in themselves sufficient to contain the forces of its desire.

Lacan's account of the split subject is radical because it rejects any principle of immanent order, or homeostasis, that might confer natural equilibrium on its inner tensions. No amount of pleasure can fully quench its desires because it only exists by desiring. It never ends up restored to perfect health or back on some 'normal' course of development. As we have seen, that is not the goal of therapy according to Lacan. The subject may well emerge from therapeutic analysis better aware of its symptoms and equipped to manage them, but subjectivity as such is not inclined to the pursuit of health and happiness. Rather, its desiring disposition compels it beyond pleasurable satisfaction altogether. To be a subject is to be situated always at the *limits* of satisfaction, that is, to experience dissatisfaction as the driving force of one's desires. At work here is not the 'pleasure principle' of Freud's early work but what in his later writings he refers to as the 'death drive'. The Lacanian account of the subject finds its central motif in this rather mysterious notion and, as I shall suggest in the section that follows, it is from the logic of the death drive that a psychopolitical approach to speech ought to proceed. First, however, let me clarify what the notion means for Lacan's subject.

In Freud's later work – most famously *Beyond the Pleasure Principle* of 1920 – the term death drive was employed to describe a startling tendency found, in certain patients, not to maximise pleasure but to direct aggression against themselves (see SE18: 7–64). Freud discovered this in victims of war-neuroses who repeatedly dreamed of returning to horrific moments of destruction. Against the logic of the pleasure principle, upon which he had till then established his programme of psychoanalysis, Freud speculated on the existence of an unconscious counter-tendency, or drive, to bring the subject towards its own organic death (see Boothby, 1991: 2–6). At the time, Freud regarded this tendency as a possible explanation for aggression towards oneself and others. However, the death drive was never satisfactorily developed by Freud and was often regarded by his followers as a curious deviation in his meta-psychology (Boothby, 1991: 6–10).

For Lacan, however, the death drive is central to psychoanalysis and to the theory of the subject he develops (Boothby, 1991: 10–20). It describes not a tendency towards organic death but, rather, how the unconscious repeatedly attacks its own psychic organisation – in particular, its imaginary ego – in order to extend its desire. As Richard Boothby explains, Lacan's understanding of the death drive is not of a counterforce to the pleasure principle but, fundamentally, is complicit with the underlying tendency of the drive: 'The erotic and destructive instincts', Boothby claims, 'are not essentially different forces' (1991: 95). Whereas the pleasure principle satisfies the drive indirectly by the mechanism of the ego, the death drive seeks the same end of satisfaction by breaking down the ego's restrictions. 'Death' here denotes 'a challenge not to the biological organism but to the structure of the ego' against whose 'repressive strictures' a struggle is 'waged by that portion of organismic energies that have remained excluded by it' (1991: 96).

The ego, as we have noted, functions as a barrier to excitation by energies felt as threatening and so screened out. Because the ego foregrounds the self as an image of integrated unity in a body that is entirely its own, what it excludes is usually experienced as a danger to its integrity, for instance in the form of dreams or fantasies of horror, destruction and dismemberment: 'what is in this way refused and remaindered in the constitution of the ego assumes the aspects of utter opacity, of uncanny, unthinkable otherness' (Boothby, 1991: 65). The death drive therefore alerts us to the salience of the register of the real over the imaginary and the pressure it constantly exerts on the ego. This pressure is present, for example, as an inexplicable tendency to 'self-sabotage' by violent imaginings that are otherwise considered illicit or destructive. The subject's unconscious, then, is in conflict with its own ego when organic energies seek satisfaction by disrupting its imagined self.

In Boothby's interpretation, the Lacanian subject is propelled by this inner discordance perpetually either to defend or relinquish the closed form of its imaginary ego. In the latter case, satisfaction comes via the releasing experience of 'enjoyment', or *jouissance*. This is an intense 'pleasure-in-pain' that is felt when a bounded image of the ego dissolves and a repressed desire to think or feel something previously refused is unleashed. It is perhaps most prosaically encountered in the form of jokes, or even insults, when a thought or idea that is normally refused acceptance by the structure of the ego suddenly arrives (in the form of a pun, perhaps), surprising the auditor with impressive economy in evading the censoriousness of the ego. Enjoyment must here be distinguished from mere pleasure, which is the compromised satisfaction achieved by trading off unconscious desire with social conventions or the practicalities of survival – such as trying to explain a joke, which makes a point in a more circuitous (and usually unfunny) way. Whereas pleasure is a limited satisfaction that permits egos to endure as they are, enjoyment releases the underlying drive energy, blocked by the ego, that propels all our desires. When we enjoy, we are at odds with an image of ourselves. As J-D Nasio argues, in the economy of desire, 'pleasure' describes satisfaction in lowering organic tension, but 'enjoyment' is the satisfaction that 'consists in the maintenance or intense augmentation of tension' (Nasio, 2001: 50–51). Since the ego is the source of one's body image, enjoyment is often experienced in types of bodily exposure or physical risk where one's corporeal integrity is thrillingly endangered. However, such enjoyment is typically socially unacceptable on any larger scale because it dissolves or evades the barriers that enable us to repress desire and live as self-contained individuals. As a consequence, the subject, for Lacan, is usually compelled to 'sublimate' its death drive by way of language.

We will pursue more of this argument in the next chapter. But, for now, it is sufficient to note that, in Lacan's theory, the subject is founded on the logic of the death drive, which means the imaginary, symbolic and real registers are constantly in mutual tension, not harmony. Psychic life is propelled not by the singular urge to liberate or maximise libidinal pleasure but by a greater urge to sabotage its own structures of organisation. It is not hedonism but masochism that describes the force of the unconscious, that is, it is an aggressiveness against the self (which may even be inverted as a sadistic attack on others) (see Boothby, 1991: 40–41). Why might this be so? Because the encounter with organic tension is itself profoundly satisfying, even if it is dangerous in any sustained form. But it is not a satisfaction in the routine type of pleasure – the kind of compromised pleasure that aligns one with social conventions, like passing exams – but an enjoyment that derives from the invocation of trauma. In the unbinding of the imaginary ego, subjects fulfil what Todd McGowan describes as 'an impetus to return to an originally traumatic and constitutive loss' (McGowan, 2013: 13). The pressure of the pure drive (or the real) produces satisfaction not in the positive realisation of acceptable pleasures but in the traumatic experience of losing one's very sense of self. For it is the wholly encompassing, if momentary, dissatisfaction in relinquishing one's psychic integrity that approximates the subject's assumption of an original and nourishing sense of corporeal wholeness. The loss of the original, privileged object – the mythical mother figure – that the child undergoes as it enters the symbolic order is constantly re-experienced in later life as an unconscious urge to recall a moment of trauma. McGowan continues: 'Though it seems completely counterintuitive, the subject enjoys the disappearance of its privileged object; it enjoys not having it rather than having it because this experience returns the subject closer to the privileged object than at any other time' (McGowan, 2013: 38).

Of course, this original loss is mythical. It is an imaginary harmony that was never experienced as such since it would have existed before the subject regarded itself as a discrete individual. But from the perspective of a subject now integrated into the symbolic order the 'lost' fullness appears as a state of harmony that has been cruelly sacrificed. Although Lacan suggests that the subject keeps trying to return to this moment, to approximate in the repeated experience of total loss a sensation of total fullness, it is a condition that never existed and never will exist. Indeed, even the enjoyment of loss is difficult to endure since it invokes what is effectively the destruction of the subject. Nonetheless, Lacan's theory presents the 'lure' of enjoyment as a constant compulsion. Though the 'lost object' is experienced in many different ways and to different degrees in each person, it describes an underlying force towards self-destruction that compels all subjects not to satisfy their desires but, moreover, to enjoy their dissatisfaction.

To say that we are driven somehow to enjoy our dissatisfaction is not as odd as it may seem. We do not enjoy in the sense of consciously delighting about loss. Rather, we enjoy by feeling ineluctably inclined to foreground the obstacles to the achievement of our desires. Enjoying, in this sense, is an unconscious undercurrent that pulls us away from the targets of our desire even as we aim at them. The barriers to desire come into focus more readily than the objects themselves, and we are thereby excited by a promise that lies beyond them. The imaginary and symbolic structures of our individual and collective psychic lives are thus tinged with an awareness of their own incompleteness or insufficiency. For McGowan, the death drive, as elaborated in the Lacanian concept of the real, explains a variety of phenomena such as a pervasive cultural nostalgia, which inclines us to think that society was once so much better or that an original 'purity' has been surrendered. But it also accounts for our readiness to political paranoia or conspiracy theories that elaborate tales of how the integrity of society has been undone by the machinations of groups or individuals 'behind the scenes' of the symbolic order and whose secret intervention prevents us from fulfilling our desires (see McGowan, 2013: 39–49). Indeed, McGowan, describes a variety of figures of loss – from images of sacrifice to religious commitment and ideological fantasies – that instantiate different formulations of the lost object in contemporary life.

Lacan's theory of the subject gives some clarity to Freud's understanding of the appeal of plausible stories. What is at work in the subject's psychic organisation is a complex process of managing the forces of unconscious bodily drives, redirecting and evading the pressure they exert upon the perceptual integrity of the ego. Psychoanalysis – but Lacanian psychoanalysis in particular – invites us to conceive subjectivity as the ongoing management of encounters with forces that provoke and threaten desire. The subject is in constant struggle with itself and so the stories it adopts to situate itself (its claims to knowledge, its theories or its explanations) appeal because they help figure the fugitive forces within it, perhaps even at the cost of its own interests, explicit beliefs, or personal well-being. This all amounts to a concept of the subject as a contradictory and inconsistent entity, driven by the force of its desire and not by an urge to know the truth of its motivations (McGowan, 2013: 17–18). But it is an idea of the subject, however, that I want to suggest is of use to rhetorical enquiry.

Rhetoric, Desire and the Lost Object

We are now in a position to make some preliminary remarks about how a psychoanalytic conception of desire relates to speech and rhetoric. The sketch of Lacan's work given above – and, in particular, the primacy given to the notion of the death drive – suggests that the subject has a contradictory relation to its desire. As a subject of language, it is compelled to desire by way of the Other, that is, by aligning its ego with the symbolic Law that simultaneously imposes prohibitions on it: desire and the Law are not opposed but inextricably linked. Yet neither the subject's own imaginary ego nor its symbolic mandate is sufficient to channel or contain the force of its drives. There is always a remainder of desire that goes unsatisfied and this surplus – in the form of the death drive – distorts the subject's relation to its imaginary and symbolic registers. We will explore the distortion brought by this excess in the next chapter. For now, we should note that, as a means to articulate our demands and public values, speech and language function at a number of psychic levels: as a medium to coordinate subjective desire *and* as a means to manage our enjoyment.

(1) In the first instance, Lacanian theory directs us to the ways rhetoric operates as a symbolic system to invoke the desire of the subject. Because the subject is split, that is, divided off from its unconscious, language provides a medium through which to express desire. This is achieved by way of signifiers that target a multiplicity of objects. Caught up in the network of signifiers, the subject achieves in speech (that is, its own and that of others) a degree of symbolic mastery. But although this enables it to overcome the paranoid duality of its narcissistic ego, symbolic systems always gravitate towards a certain alienating order. That is to say, language involves a pact with the Other. To speak and to hear speech is to construct one's desire via the Other that functions as the locus of truth in our discourse. Whether instantiated in an actual figure or principle, or simply an implied one, the Other is the assumed source of the authority in our claims and demands. It is a 'phallic' principle representing symbolic mastery that we take for granted but which nonetheless validates our speech. It need not be embodied in an actual person nor even in the direct interlocutor of our discourse. Symbolic authority is an unconsciously assumed perspective *from which* validation flows. In everyday discourse, the Other may be embodied, for example, by a principle of good government, the law, common sense, or whatever those in power may say. As a locus, the purpose of the Other is to stitch together signifiers and guarantee the validity of our speech, rather than to say anything in particular. So we usually end up arguing (as we do in law courts, legislative assemblies, and bars) about what the Other really wants. Public speech and rhetoric thus elaborate symbolic pathways to invoke the authority of the Other.

Rhetoric facilitates the 'metonymic' movement of desire by offering alternate pathways for speech to connect signifiers by displacing meaning along symbolic chains joining them to the Other (see Lacan, 2006: 421). The classical rhetorical appeals to reason, character, and emotion (the celebrated figures of *logos, ethos* and *pathos*), for example, project psycholinguistic pathways to the symbolic authority of the Other in so far as they guarantee the truth of our discourse. That way, our voices become vehicles to conjoin desires to an authority that always goes beyond them. Speaking desires is thus a contradictory experience because it involves inserting them into a medium that separates them from us in order to validate them. As psychoanalyst, Massimo Recalcati, puts it: 'the experience of desire is simultaneously mine and not mine; a property and improper; an immanence and a transcendence' (Recalcati, 2014: 12). To speak one's desires is, if only implicitly, to request recognition from the Other but also, therefore, to be vulnerable to its refusal or indifference.

(2) Public speech may operate primarily in a symbolic register but – outside of purely formal, bureaucratic discourse – it rarely escapes the impact of the real. As a psychical function, the Other never fully reveals itself and, in its objective forms (in authority figures and institutions, for example), only infrequently demonstrates a consistency or competence that matches its symbolic function. We are, therefore, always compelled to ask what the law demands, what God wants from us, how much do my demands align with what society expects of me, and so on. Anxious uncertainty about the Other is how the force of the real is typically felt, suggesting that all persuasive discourse circulates around *pathos*, which originally refers to grief or suffering. As suggested above, the real is disclosed as an obsession with the 'lost object', a missing fullness that channels discourse towards an intensity of feeling that roots the strictures of the symbolic order in something beyond it. The key rhetorical occasions in classical times, for example, were when citizens confronted the prospect of collective death, bodily sacrifice or personal disadvantage – situations where we must ask what the Other wants or, more precisely, what it is that it *enjoys*. To face the prospect of loss, public speech addresses collective dissatisfaction by enjoying it. Military defeat must be faced with the urge for 'glory', economic and political disaster with a sense of 'love' for the polis, and legal defeat with an attitude of the overriding virtue of 'justice'. Although they imply dissatisfaction and often personal sacrifice, these terms invest the Other with corporeal qualities that invite citizens to secretly enjoy their loss. Beneath the surface demands of our speech,

which seem aimed at concrete satisfaction, lurks a contrary, unconscious urge to imagine their dissatisfaction (see, for example, Millar, 2006).

Reflection on rhetoric itself, it has been noted, has long been prone to nostalgia (see Garsten, 2006: 14–15). Speakers and speeches in the past are regularly invoked in the present as markers of a noble world of civic-mindedness, now eclipsed. Lamenting the supposed 'decline' of eloquence, especially in its classical form, is a persistent tendency in modern writing on public life. Here, rhetoric as such – often itself labelled as the 'lost art' – becomes a privileged medium for the urge to revel in the enjoyment of some absent dignity, usually neglecting the point that 'oratory and eloquence arose only in tumultuous times when gifted speakers could draw angry or frightened people into partisan mobs' (Garsten, 2006: 15). Symbolic authority nonetheless seems more appealing when associated with the ghostly qualities of a bygone era of statesmen who transcended mere struggles for power.

(3) My contention is that public speech invites auditors to identify symbolically, in order to organise their desire, and also to manage their enjoyment. But it is important to underline that we are concerned here with *public* speech, which is directed at general and diverse audiences and at desire as such, not with the personal ailments of specific individuals. This is a significant difference with the clinical setting of discourse that psychoanalysts, such as Lacan, mostly deal with. My concern is not with decoding the intimate conversations between patients and analysts (on which, see Fink, 1999 and Baldwin, 2015). Public speech is – perhaps like cinema, literature, or other cultural forms – something of which we usually choose to make ourselves audiences, not only when we are compelled by distress or illness. The 'plausible stories' proffered by public speakers – by politicians, lawyers, intellectuals, preachers, or cultural commentators, among others – are discourses directed *at* us, and not always produced *by* us. They compete to capture our attention and offer narratives, formulate arguments, and supply repeatable phrases that we may eventually take as our own. But we should beware treating audiences of rhetorical discourse as recip-

ients of therapy. Public speech largely conforms to the conventional repertoires and strategies of certain kinds of institutional practice and the dilemmas they face and not to the singular habits and concerns of specific individuals.

Nor is it my concern to 'psychoanalyse' speakers or explore in depth their motivating intentions. Increasingly, public speakers are not the authors of their own words (they employ a speech writer or even a team of writers). Effective public speech – whether in set-piece speeches or wider deliberations – is not to be judged strictly from the author or performer's point of view but from the way it captures forces never entirely in anyone's command. Like other cultural practices, public speech relies upon a general capacity to desire. Speakers aim to capture often confused or uncoordinated energies by giving them symbolic shape and direction. The plausible stories of public culture are in constant circulation as efforts to mobilise publics and fashion temporary, rather than lasting, political attachments.

Conclusion

In this chapter I have begun to deepen the question, raised in Chapter 1, about how rhetoric may be conceived as an embodied practice. To do this I have drawn upon psychoanalytic theory to understand subjectivity as a complex whole. From this (admittedly schematic) perspective, speech and argument are the medium through which a discordant subject manages its unconscious desires and the organic impulses that propel it. Subjectivity, then, denotes not a fully-conscious, rational agency wholly in charge of itself but a fractured and conflictual body of competing psychic forces. For that reason, an approach to rhetoric that draws upon psychoanalysis differs radically from one that draws upon psychology: subjectivity is not an arrangement of independent mental processes functioning separately from the wider body but, rather, an unstable fusion of forces whose unity is never secured. The psychoanalytical subject is always on the verge of existential crisis as it struggles to find coherence through systems that nonetheless alienate it, making selfhood radically dependent upon others (images and symbols) that it never takes fully as its own. In this framework, public speech and argument do not figure simply as portable devices to enhance communication between self-aware agents. Rather, they operate as a medium through which subjects constitute themselves and their worlds by activating desires and managing enjoyment.

3. Talking to Excess

In the last chapter I suggested that Lacan offers a framework for understanding notable psychical dimensions of public speech. For him, language is a signifying activity through which subjectivity is partly constituted and not just a means of communication between fully formed egos. Speaking – and other forms of cultural and symbolic discourse – involves activating pathways along which corporeal energies are projected, targeting named objects of desire, and attaching the subject to the Other by its submission to various conventions and prohibitions. What propels this subject, however, is a drive whose satisfaction is achieved only at the expense of the imaginary ego. I indicated that, for Lacan, the unsymbolised excess of energy he categorises as the 'real' is frequently experienced as a peculiarly destructive enjoyment in the dissolution of the ego's boundaries. Such enjoyment cannot be directly endured so takes a symbolic form, providing indirect satisfaction by invoking the presence of a lost object that approximates a primordial fullness. All subjects must manage their desires in light of this alluring but also threatening urge. Rhetorical discourse, I submit, is a vital means to manage it.

In this chapter I want to explore further the idea of an excess at the heart of subjectivity. In particular, I want to defend the view that speech is a medium for managing that excess by transforming it into a mechanism to stimulate and sustain desire. This brings into view the celebrated figure that Lacan named the *objet petit a* – the 'small a object' of desire. The *objet a* refers not to an empirical object but, rather, to an absence that incites desire as such by giving focus to the drive. It describes an enigmatic quality, frequently evoked in speech and argument, which is the marker of a missing enjoyment that arouses our attention. But nor is it a figure in the sense of a determinate 'figure of speech' or rhetorical device. The *objet a* may take many linguistic or cultural forms because, distinctively, its presence is one of absence. It is this peculiar figure that marks out the place of the lost object, mentioned in the last chapter, and that enables the subject to reinvest in its attachment to the Other.

Incorporating the *objet a* into our discussion permits us better to understand how desire is provoked and managed discursively. Public and political speech is never fully contained by formal rules and conventions. Rather, it responds to, or encircles, the presence of something that exceeds it. An indeterminate locus of intensity, this something evokes anxiety and distress if it cannot be grasped symbolically. An inaccessible 'thing', it is often registered metaphorically, rather than directly described, so as to be apprehended in language. The inventiveness of rhetoric stems from the effort to transform this dangerous excess into language, shifting or tilting our perceptual horizons so that we might see things anew. Below I discuss this peculiar psychic phenomenon, first of all, in terms of the relation between perceptual 'position' and 'disposition'. I then go on to explore how it operates in the form of fantasy before claiming that the *objet a* offers insight into the way a 'rhetorical situation' provokes discourse. Finally, I suggest that this excess is often presented visually in political rhetoric as a 'stain' on the horizon that serves to incite our passions.

Seeing Things Anew

We tend to see more than we consciously notice. In our visual field there is always far more detail than we can possibly apprehend. Inevitably, then, visual perception – like perception in general – is a matter of directing attention at some aspects of a field while relegating others to the margins. Sometimes that means we pay no attention to what may be directly before us; or we may pay acute amounts of attention to minor details that, at least to others, have no great bearing. Rhetoric, I want to argue, can be conceived as a means to direct and focus our attention and persuasion can thus be understood as a process of 'seeing things anew'. Sometimes that might feel like having a whole new perception of an object or it may involve simply viewing it in a slightly modified light so that it stands out more. However dramatic or subtle the experience, the process involves us finding ourselves before an idea, object or feeling and grasping something new or different in it.

The function of rhetoric, then, can be conceived as one of modifying the way we experience and organise our perceptions. By figuring language, what is represented is held in a certain light, given associative connection to other things, and thereby made relevant to us in distinct ways. The shapes (or figures) of language – its linguistic and conceptual arrangements and styles – disclose a world to audiences in ways that 'throw light' on certain parts, illuminating some aspects and withdrawing others, if only partially, from view. For this reason, rhetoric has accurately been described as an 'art of positionality in address', that is, a skill of establishing a determinate stance on an issue, often against an opposing view, by posing it in a particular way (Bender and Wellbery, 1990: 7). But if, at one level, rhetoric helps position us towards the world of objects then, at another, it also undertakes the unconscious task of 'disposition', that is, of rendering a field of experience perceptible in a such a way that a position seems appropriate to adopt.

This distinction between 'position' and 'disposition' is useful for thinking about the way speech operates rhetorically and psychically at the same time. For if rhetoric concerns how language disposes us to the world argumentatively, psychoanalysis similarly concerns the way the unconscious disposes the subject to its sense of self. As Richard Boothby (whose work I will draw upon closely in this section) argues, Freud's innovation is comparable to other phenomenological philosophies in the early twentieth century – such as those of Heidegger or Merleau-Ponty – in demonstrating that the self-aware ego and its relation to the world is made possible only by the unacknowledged presence of repressed memories or compromised wishes that, unconsciously, enable it to stand out in the field of its experience as a distinct and bounded 'centre' to perception and judgement (see Boothby, 2001). For Boothby, Lacan's thought gives greater precision to this thesis, particularly by clarifying the function of language in disposing the perceptual field. But, first, let me explore the rhetorical dimension to perception.

The concepts of position and disposition might best be grasped initially by way of Gestalt psychology. This approach sought to describe fundamental principles in the organisation of perception that were understood to function by relating particular elements of experience to their wider field (see Boothby, 2001: 37–43). Perhaps the most well known (and fundamental) of its distinctions was that between 'figure' and 'ground': an isolated figure can be visually perceived only by virtue of relating it to and distinguishing it from the broader context surrounding it – for example, the way a single tree might stand out in a clearing against an empty background. The way any perceptual figure appears to us (that is, how it is positioned with a perceptible contour that separates it off) is determined by its relation to an environing ground (its dispositional field) that recedes into the background. On a purely visual level, this effect is noticed in images such as Rubin's Vase which, depending on how we focus our attention, depicts either a white vase against a black background or two silhouetted faces against a white background. What is striking here is that both figures cannot be seen at once. One figure can be discerned only when the other recedes into an indeterminate surround.

The notions of figure and ground in Gestalt psychology demonstrate how even simple visual perception entails the relational articulation of phenomena, isolating and accentuating certain figures by diminishing others and thereby foregrounding some visual relations at the expense of others that are held off (and yet remain available if, as in the case of Rubin's vase, we shift our focus of attention). Gestalt theory tries to account for the most common modes of organising perception into coherent, regular shapes. This approach was highly influential on Merleau-Ponty, who took the figure-ground concept as a model for his work on the body and its schemas (see Boothby, 2001: 54–61; Dillon, 1997: 58–81). But the process is not exclusive to visual perception. Cognition can also be said to be structured the same way in so far as conscious reasoning is organised via patterns and relations, or 'schemata', that enable boundaries to coalesce around conceptual figures. Indeed, conceptual thinking has close affinities to visual perception (see Arnheim, 1997). We can see that figures of speech, or tropes, in rhetoric enable inner 'ways of seeing' that accentuate certain perceptual features and relations over others. The 'standing-outness', as Tucker (2001) puts it, of particular rhetorical qualities – or what Chaïm Perelman (1982) calls 'presence' in rhetorical argument – is achieved by forms of speech that selectively connect, highlight and diminish aspects of their content. Tropes and schemes, for example, give shape to both the arrangement of words and/or concepts in a way that mirrors visual organisation. In short, rhetoric organises concepts into patterns of difference and association that dispose us towards phenomena such that we position ourselves accordingly.

Baruchello (2015), for example, classifies the major rhetorical tropes according to distinct Gestalt principles, such as the 'law of symmetry' or the 'law of proximity' (see 2015: 12). The first identifies structural patterns across similarly repeated elements, whereas the second finds a pattern in elements brought together. Rhetorical examples of symmetry include 'anaphora' (the repetition of the same words in successive clauses or sentences, which produces emphasis by way of recurrence). For example, Winston Churchill, in a well-known statement of 1940 to the Commons underlined his determination: 'We shall fight on the beaches, we shall fight on the landing grounds, we shall fight on the fields and in the streets, we shall fight in the hills; we shall never surrender' (Churchill, 2007: 171). Proximity, on the other hand, can be found in 'tricolon' (three words or ideas expressed in parallel or in a concise series, whose proximity to each other creates an implicit connection). For example, President Obama's opening lines in his 2009 Inaugural: 'I stand here today humbled by the task before us, grateful for the trust you have bestowed, mindful of the sacrifices borne by our ancestors' (Obama, 2009). Even if these patterns are broken, the breach can have a dissonant effect that impacts upon thought precisely because it undermines the coherence that tropes normally offer.

How, then, does psychoanalysis add to our understanding of rhetorical position and disposition? Simply put, it suggests that what is at work in speech and argument is how the subject organises its desires. Rhetoric doesn't just shape the way we think and form conceptual judgements – that is, processes of cognition. It also has a deeper, *affective* impact on how the cognising subject coordinates the various parts of its psyche through which, as we have seen, its desire is manifest (Frosh, 1989: 133). This is why rhetoric often provokes us to feel, as well as to understand, disposing us to reason in particular ways. While not disputing the cognitive dimension to rhetoric, the psychoanalytical assumption of an unconscious implies that language and symbols give presence to deeper and unacknowledged aspects of desire whilst simultaneously holding off others. In that respect, 'seeing things anew' involves positioning one's ego by taking up a distinctive rhetorical stance. We respond differently, for example, to the arrival in our midst of strangers if they are described as 'hard working individuals looking for employment' than if they are presented as 'refugees of war-torn countries needy of our assistance'.

Richard Boothby (2001) argues, in a rich and stimulating analysis, that Lacan's insights about language and subjectivity can be understood in terms of the distinction between positional and dispositional processes. For Lacan, as we have seen, the self – or, properly, the ego – is an imaginary object, an internalised image on whose surface the subject attaches its desires. The subject positions itself by identifying with this image, which then permits it to relate other objects to it. But the image is fundamentally alienating and unstable: it derives from a misperceived external image (in the mirror) that leads the subject to assume (despite its own experience of fragmentation) the intrinsic unity and autonomy of its bodily self. The importance of the imaginary ego in the subject's development lies, as we have seen, in supplying a constant and dependable location from which to filter desires, enabling it to exclude disagreeable feelings that seem to threaten its integrity. In turn, that allows it to regard the world as an orderly arrangement of enclosed, bounded objects like itself. But the positionality of this ego – the firmness of its contours, which separate it from other objects, and its inner homogeneity – is persistently exposed, as we saw in our discussion of the death drive, to the unbinding forces of the real. If we are unable to discriminate our hardworking individuals from our needy refugees, to continue the example, we may not satisfactorily grasp our own position towards them and so feel unaccountably threatened.

In Lacan's analysis, argues Boothby, it is language – or the symbolic register – that resolves the tendency to aggression and paranoia that assails the subject. How is this achieved? In taking up language and entering into ever wider networks of social relations the subject learns to diminish its investment in a rigidly fixed self-image and attach itself instead to signifiers. Language functions in the unconscious as a dispositional field by exposing the subject to the open play of signifying differences, whose multiple forms qualify and enrich its experience. In so doing, the ego's tendency to fixate its desires on static images is displaced by a network of signifiers whose perpetual interconnections and differentiations are highly fluid. Where this process of submitting desire to language halts is frequently where psychic illness starts: 'it is not difficult to recognize many of the typical signatures of neurosis – the phobia, the compulsive idea, the hysterical identification – as situations in which the fluid potentiality of the symbolic has been pooled and frozen in the hollows of imaginary formations' (Boothby, 2001: 122). By contrast, in effectively aligning our desire with the desire of the symbolic Other, we learn to live in a constant but relievable tension between the imaginary and symbolic registers – between the composite images we have of our integrity as a coherent self and the constant extensions and delays to our desires that language imposes. The psychoanalytic practice of the talking cure – and especially the method of 'free association' – aims, therefore, to suspend the tendency to what Boothby calls 'imaginary agglutination', when subjects dwell on totalizing images, so as to dissolve them in the solution of language (2001: 118–19).

In contrast to the imaginary, whose images position the subject within relatively fixed boundaries, signifiers disassemble the firmness of imaginary contours and maintain an openness to difference that images cannot. Because signifiers are never pure presences but always invoke something absent, and because they can be infinitely reordered and supplemented, adding and removing associations as they are extended, they hold open the possibility of refiguring otherwise unacceptable thoughts and ideas. In Lacan's approach to language, the interconnection and mutual recombination of signifiers displaces any finality of meaning along chains that are only ever arbitrarily closed (by coming to a conclusion). Symbols extend, qualify and re-contextualise desires rather than condense them into one closed image. We learn thus to acknowledge certain feelings, accept the presence of people we once thought threatening, or to recognise parts of our personalities that we once refused. Such openness is never entirely arbitrary (since there are rules in any language that impose some regularity of some kind) but it is fluid in a way that images are not. As Boothby says, 'words possess primary meanings that are girt about by a range of incomplete tendrils of inchoate significance' (2001: 126). Speech and language hold out the possibility of weakening the boundaries enclosing the subject's imaginary ego, that symbolic associations and differences can soften the rigidity of a self-image. That way, it becomes possible to talk around unacceptable desires, to rephrase them and signify them in ways that capture some of their force, without simply accepting or rejecting them wholesale. This is a work of 'sublime violence', according to Boothby (2001: 160). Signifiers function on the side of desire against the ego, unbinding its rigid imaginary unity and finding new ways to access the real.

What happens in the symbolic register, then, is akin to the Gestalt shift mentioned above. The subject comes to figure its ego anew, perhaps by diminishing parts of it and enhancing others. As a refigured ego, it also relates to other objects in new ways. Symbolic structures supply an impersonal position from which we can see ourselves – rather than exclusively from inside our own paranoid egos. Just as, for example, religion invites us to view things from the perspective of a God who observes and judges our conduct, so different formations of the Other position the ego in ways that encourage the enhancement of some qualities, relations, or aspects of ourselves over others. 'Symbolic identification' with the Other offers a position within a structure from which we may reflect – often critically – on how we personally match up to the ideal point of view of the Other. In Boothby's argument, Lacan encourages us to regard the registers of the imaginary and symbolic as being in constant tension as the ego's positional stance is perpetually caught up in the 'defiles of the signifer'. What is important here is that the symbolic doesn't simply give us reasons – that is, ways to cognitively process – but, moreover, it alters the unconscious perspective (or stance) *from which* we reason. Which is why, we might assume, sometimes we resist arguments that pull us in to their reasoning because they challenge our sense of who we are, the parameters of our empathy, and so where we stand on a matter. More than a device for shaping reasoning, the symbolic dimension of arguments pressure us to give up something of our self-image and thereby threaten to reshape our personal integrity. That is often a discomforting experience because it challenges the implicit picture of who we are and how we align our attachments and commitments, which we often like to think all converge in a seamless and unified whole.

Perhaps it is this powerful sense of displacing and repositioning personal and social identity through argument that makes religious sermonising an exemplary model for rhetorical persuasion. For the arguments of preachers are often directed firmly at the vulnerabilities of the ego, offering a symbolic point of reference in the Divine from which to weaken its autonomy and centrality for the subject. For example, to give oneself up to Christ – to undergo conversion – is manifestly to undertake a Gestalt shift, to start seeing the world radically anew and to rediscover one's place in it. Much religious rhetoric is at times unashamedly hyperbolic, staking its claim to reveal its truth on the basis of exaggerated figures – such as 'God is love' – that contrast markedly with everyday speech (see Webb, 1993). And it does this so that our previous way of looking at things can only be conceived as defective or unintelligible. More precisely, it inscribes one's desires not exclusively in the ego but by way of the Other. Of course, the ego remains, but it is much diminished as it diverts the subject's desire around new symbolic chains that position it differently. Not all rhetoric is aimed at producing this kind of transformative effect, not even religious rhetoric. Indeed, most is directed at only slight or localised adjustments, or even none at all. A good part of public debate generally might even be said to be aimed *not* at deliberately challenging people's self-images but at reinforcing them. But the conversion experience – when the world suddenly seems different and the subject feels itself emboldened by a new and refreshed sense of self – is perhaps a limit case of rhetorical persuasion fulfilling the function of the death drive. The old ego dissolves and a new one, adjusted to new symbolic coordinates, takes its place.

Fantasy and Excess

Staged within rhetorical argumentation, then, is a relation – often a tense one – between symbolic and imaginary dimensions of the subject and the way it represents its own desires. But, as Boothby further reminds us, the dialectic of position/disposition goes beyond this binary relation. For the underlying ground of the subject – the site at which this contest between imaginary and symbolic is fought – is the question of what the Other wants. What compels the subject – the reason it is prepared to challenge or even sabotage its ego – is an urge to figure out what its fundamentally unrepresentable desire is and how it relates it to the Other. As Boothby explains, the unknowable character of desire unfolds in perceptual encounters as 'an unencompassable aspect of every representation' (2001: 204). There is always something more in what we experience that we cannot fully grasp. Likewise, in all public situations we encounter the mysterious question of what it is that is wanted of us, although a final answer remains permanently out of reach. The dialectic of position and disposition thus emerges out of an original trauma that, thereafter, haunts the subject as an underlying excess in the organisation of its desire. Although, as I have argued above, speech and language give form to some of this energy, nonetheless a quantity remains that cannot be assimilated. This surplus, or excess, according to Lacan is figured as fantasy.

Let me unravel this argument in a little more detail before clarifying how it relates to our discussion of rhetoric. As we have seen, in Lacan's theory, the subject emerges originally from a separation from the original Other, often the mother figure, in whose gaze the infant first forms its imaginary ego. The subject initially perceives itself as the object of the (m)Other's desire. But, as the child matures, it struggles to discern what the Other wants from it, especially when it has alternative attractions (such as, for example, the father). Eventually, as we noted, the child comes to seek the recognition of the Other symbolically – that is, by way of social structures and mechanisms that require it to relinquish its inflated, narcissistic sense of self. But the pressure to find this lost relation to the Other remains as an underlying 'gravitational' pull in all its subsequent activities. Following Freud, Lacan initially refers to this force of attraction as 'the Thing' *(das Ding)*: '*Das Ding* is that which I call the beyond-of-the-signified' (1992: 54). It is a figure that represents, not the mother as such, but a mysterious dimension unconsciously encountered in all objects, an uncanny or excessive presence that connects the imaginary to the real. Objects, such as people or places, when encountered for the first time are usually assimilated to what we already know but they always contain a specificity that we do not recognise. Boothby understands the Thing as a means to denote this 'unrecognizable surplus in perception' (2001: 207). As we encounter objects in different situations, the question of what we are in relation to those objects – or, more precisely, what they want from us – is unconsciously posed as an echo of that original, imaginary relation to the Other that once affirmed our desire. The Thing, then, designates the enigmatic quality of an object that stands simultaneously for the unknowability of the subject's own, real desire.

What, so far, I have been referring to as the pressure of the real is experienced less as a series of random organic impulses excluded from conscious symbolisation and more as a questioning around the subject's perceptual frame. Until we find answers to that question (by way of the symbolic register) we remain disoriented and profoundly unsettled by some experiences – because, as Boothby puts it, 'they excite an unrepresentable dimension of the subject's own desire' (2001: 208). Uncanny situations (where something appears that seems out of place) return us to an original traumatic experience of uncertainty and loss that exceeds the capacity of our ego to assert control. Put another way, in the presence of the Thing, we experience 'the real core around which the unity of the imaginary is wrapped' (2001: 211). Although it is encountered as something unknowable, 'out there' in the world that we perceive, it is within our own intimate sense of selfhood – the bounded ego that is constructed so as to discriminate what belongs to it and what does not – that this uncanny experience dramatically unfolds. That is why we often feel both delight and trepidation at things we cannot quite see or fully experience. Falling in love, for instance, usually brings a fascination with the image (of our lover) and a persistent questioning over what desires lie behind the adored face. As Lacan himself claimed in his discussion of 'courtly love', behind the face of the idealised Other lies an inaccessible object that seems to summon us (Lacan, 1992: 145–54). What we are attracted to, however, is something beyond pleasure, a fulfilment that threatens to dissolve the bounded unity of the ego. That is why we are sometimes prepared to sacrifice ourselves for the affection we hold for certain objects (such as a lover or one's country).

It is this unrepresentable dimension of experience that fundamentally animates language and connects the dialectic of position and disposition to the Other. Signifiers help to designate the initially overflowing excess that the Thing presents. They are motivated by the absence of containment in the object that is the Thing. Words never fully capture all its qualities but, instead, circle around it, naming aspects of it but never exhausting its abundance. The dispositional role we have attributed to speech thus supplies what Boothby calls an 'indeterminate positionality' to objects (2001: 218), giving presence to some aspects over others, and holding open the possibility of further articulation.

Lacan's reference to an unknowable dimension external to language is later developed into an idea of something beyond symbolisation that is nonetheless present *in* language. This is the basis to his idea of fantasy, or what he also refers to as the *objet petit a* (small a object) or the 'object cause of desire'. Normally, fantasy is understood to be an outlandish scenario in which magical things seem possible. But for Lacan fantasy organises our everyday perceptions by figuring the excess of desire – presented above as the inaccessible Thing – as a stable frame through which symbolic and imaginary tensions are smoothed over and given a degree of consistency. Where the Thing denoted a dimension of experience that remained inaccessible and sits on the margins of the imaginary, fantasy describes a way of incorporating that inaccessible element into the symbolic. It enables us to invest our desires in a way of looking at (and thereby bodily inhabiting) the world.

The *objet a* is called the 'object cause of desire' because it stimulates the subject's desire (rather than its anxiety) by signalling something lacking whose restoration promises satisfaction. It is not a discrete object that can be directly represented but, rather, the blurred marker of absence itself. Stemming from the early experiences of objects ceded by the subject as an infant (the breast, faeces, etc) it has a liminal existence between subjectivity and objectivity: it is both an intense presence but also an absence (see Lacan, 1977: 103–4). To be an autonomous subject at all the individual must cede these objects to the Other and yet it retains an attachment to them as the lacking source of intimate bodily experiences that evoke direct enjoyment. The *objet a* therefore embodies a profoundly contradictory experience as a locus of intensity whose presence as absence is necessary to constitute the subject in the first place. The *objet a* functions as a figure of excess that recalls both the sacrifices required to be a desiring subject and the tremendous fullness of being that it assumes it has given up. Like standing on a cliff edge, aware that one might fall into the space before us, we are simultaneously charged with an element of bodily anxiety and also the urge to encounter the prospect of losing ourselves entirely. As Boothby puts it: 'The *objet a* is the point at which the subject assumes a certain paradoxical consistency precisely by virtue of marking the impossibility of coincidence of the subject with itself' (2001: 245).

Because it excites desire rather than simply threatens the subject, the *objet a* advances beyond the anxiety provoked by the Thing and introduces a certain intensity into the symbolic realm (through which desire is signified). Such intensity endows the symbolic domain with enhanced qualities that attract the subject to an unreachable satisfaction beyond words. This is what Lacan understands as the dimension of fantasy: an absent element around which the symbolic realm is constructed which grips the subject internally as a profound source of attraction. Boothby argues that fantasy can be understood, in his terms, as a 'dispositional object': it is neither simply a figure (it cannot be directly visualised as an object) nor a ground (since it is does not merely withdraw from view); rather, it operates across the two by focusing desire on certain images and yet holding open the possibility that what is sought in the image will shift elsewhere. The common feature of fantasy is the sense that something enormously desirable is perceived in a specific object (a person, a place, a thing) that never quite coincides with the object itself: an enigmatic source of attraction seems to heighten its appeal but we never capture it if we come close.

Far from being an other-worldly experience, fantasy is vital to the discursive construction of our normal, everyday reality (Stavrakakis, 1999: 75–82). The symbolic order is rendered coherent by a fantasmatic element that frames the mystifying demands of the symbolic Other with a sense of potential or promise. The strangeness of the Other – its infuriating inconsistency, the cruel and painful demands it makes on us, its perfunctory disregard for our feelings – comes to be presented as an intelligible, even desirable quality that holds out the prospect of an otherwise elusive satisfaction. Whether in the way we idealise our professions (despite cruel workplace politics), our marriages (despite years of mutual disappointment and contempt) or political commitments (despite the scandals and atrocities undertaken in their name), fantasy functions psychically like a light source that casts upon certain objects a particular, highly compensatory hue. In so doing, it directs us away from the unfathomable dimension of desire and folds our feelings of excess into the service of the Other. In that way, the real is partly domesticated by the transformation of anxiety into the promise of anticipated fulfilment.

Lacan's notion of fantasy has been especially influential in recent work on ideology (see Žižek, 1989; Glynos, 2001). That is because it implies a kind of misdirection of attention that enhances our attachment to symbolic frameworks by investing them with qualities that invoke the prospect of a fulfilling realisation of desire. Ideology thus distracts us from the real – that is, from the glaring gaps and inconsistencies in the symbolic order that we cannot tolerate – and allows us to believe that society is (or could be) fundamentally coherent or that any problems with it derive from an external disruption. Ideology works not so much by deceiving us that something is true that isn't but by making us believe that any evident failings or inconsistencies are neither intrinsic nor eternal. For Lacan, in therapeutic analysis we should endeavour to 'traverse the fantasy', that is, to interrogate it in order to eventually relinquish its hold over our desire. That means understanding that it is our own investment, rather than something inherent, that keeps us anchored to the Other. In political terms it may mean coming to an awareness of how the symbolic order is held together by unquestioned attachments that focus our attention on highly selective images and vocabularies.

Perhaps a good example of this approach to ideological fantasy is the case of nationalism. Nationalist discourses often aim to capture desire by presenting a variety of different objects and experiences as elements of a common, underlying essence. From cultural conventions and objects such as types of clothing, food, or leisure, to certain beliefs about history, education or government: disparate elements are held to be expressions of an underlying (that is, strictly unrepresentable) and appealing national essence that endows them with a singular sense of being or even 'destiny'. Though otherwise impossible to perceive, partaking in these conventions, practices or beliefs is held to be sharing in a common promise. Nationhood is thus both everywhere and nowhere, visible in many objects and yet not exhausted by any of them. This is not some magical dreamed-up world but the perception of an everyday reality that, by virtue of this purported common substance, is nonetheless endowed with sublime qualities that allows it, on occasion, to shimmer with an intensity that exceeds its ordinariness. When called to define what this enigmatic quality is, however, it is hard to put into words in a precise way without revealing its intrinsic banality. Often it comes to down to an ineffable 'feeling' or 'a way of looking at things' that is attributed to the things themselves. This, as I have argued above, is precisely what fantasy does to our perception and understanding of experience: it permits us to see things in a distinct light that folds what feels excessive in the object into the alluring dimension of a promise.

Extimate Situations

This account of how discourse manages the excess of subjectivity can now be focussed on the more familiar territory of rhetorical enquiry. The discussion is especially relevant to the notion of the 'rhetorical situation', which refers to the specific circumstance that generates rhetoric by opening up a space of intervention. Lacan's conception of the subject as the locus of an excess that renders it amenable to fantasy expands our understanding of how such situations operate as the 'cause' of desire.

The rhetorical situation has been important in contemporary rhetorical enquiry for exploring the way speech emerges out of particular social and historical circumstances (see Martin, 2015; Turnbull, 2017). In Bitzer's famous account, rhetoric is held to be generated by a certain type of situation, a contextual scenario comprising an 'exigence' – an 'actual or potential' dilemma or problem – that invites response; an audience for whom the exigence is of import; and other 'constraints', such as prevailing conventions or beliefs, that influence the rhetor (see Bitzer, 1968: 6). Events such as social and political crises, policy failures, or catastrophes of varying scales confound routine ways of acting and create pressures for discursive intervention so that the situation might be modified. Rhetoric is thus apparently called forth by an 'objective' situation (and not simply at will) so that the exigence might be confronted and resolved, perhaps by new ways of understanding it or tackling it. A situation is rhetorical in Bitzer's view only if it is amenable to modification; and, if so, by way of audiences who are receptive to what he describes as a 'fitting response' to the dilemma thrown up by the exigence (1968: 10). Although not all situations find such a response, rhetorical discourse is essentially pragmatic, he argues, in so far as it is 'located in reality' and attends to 'objective and publicly observable historic facts in the world we experience'. That being so, such situations can be distinguished from those that are merely 'contrived', based on 'fantasy' or simply 'fictive' (1968: 11).

Bitzer's account of the rhetorical situation offers an objectivist theory of rhetoric. Rhetoric proper arises from actual, real-world problems and not fictions. Public discourse, he implies, should be taken seriously when it is a response to an independent 'reality' that calls it 'into existence' (1968: 9). The exigence that invites response is defined as 'an imperfection marked by urgency; it is a defect, an obstacle, something waiting to be done, a thing which is other than it should be' (1968: 6). Here, however, we begin to notice than an exigence is difficult to separate off as an external cause grounded in objective reality. How can a problem be both purely objective and classified as imperfect, defective, or 'other than it should be'? The latter are normative claims not neutral descriptions since they imply standards of expectation about the world. As such they fall into the rhetorical camp, to be classified as figures of speech and not as plain 'facts', which suggests that the cause in rhetorical situations cannot be so easily distinguished from its anticipated effects or actual responses. The asserted distinction between contrived and genuine situations is thus hard to maintain.

Indeed, although Bitzer asserts that the situation is so 'controlling that we should consider it the very ground of rhetorical activity' (1968: 5), his own account gradually makes the situation appear more complicated and difficult to isolate. He admits, for example, that situations can be complex, involving numerous and sometimes incompatible exigences; sometimes there is more than one situation, or the audience may be 'scattered' or 'uneducated regarding its duties and powers' (1968: 12). In short, the situation may not clearly determine a single response. Of course, we may read these qualifications as empirical variations that complicate but do not intrinsically alter the principle that situations generate rhetoric. But they do weaken the assumed causal role of an exigence on the situation and that leads other scholars to claim that different factors, such as the rhetorical skills of the speaker (see Vatz, 1973) or the persistence of prevailing rhetorical conventions (see Jamieson, 1973), reasonably contribute to the character of the exigence. That is to say, the exigence cannot be positively separated from the overall situation in order to be attributed determining significance since its impact is bound up with the rhetorical responses it provokes.

The Lacanian notion of the excessive subject, however, offers a way to think of rhetorical causality without prioritising the exigence nor, alternatively, collapsing explanation into the blurred confluence of any number of 'immanent' factors (see Rothenberg, 2010). Because the subject is incomplete or lacking, it cannot be taken as a discrete entity that, in linear fashion, is suddenly confronted by purely external events that cause it subsequently to respond (in the manner of one billiard ball bouncing into another, causing the second one to roll across the table). Rather, there is a strange temporal circularity whereby the rhetorical response itself identifies the cause that generates it. In specifying an external 'blockage' or 'defect' that prevents it from being itself, the subject is drawn into positing its own cause. For example, when a governing elite is denounced for its malevolent neglect of popular needs and wishes, 'the people' is generated as a political subject seeking satisfaction by virtue of the elite's misdeeds. The exigence (here, elite neglect) is thus *both* exterior *and* interior to the subject because the exigence has to be posited (rhetorically) as the independent cause that now gives rise to an intervention. The cause in this instance is, as Žižek puts it, 'the retroactive product of its own effects' (Žižek, 1994: 31). If we try to examine the objective features of the exigence by itself (eg contemptuous attitudes, various authoritarian judgements, corruption, and so on), there is little that appears sufficient in itself to produce such polarising effects. However, the objective cause comes into being as a substantial phenomenon by the act of symbolisation (eg rhetoric about the neglected people) that is purportedly produced by it.

This peculiar logic is what Lacan described with the neologism, 'extimacy' *(extimité)*, meaning simultaneously external and internal, or intimate, to the subject (see Miller, 2008). The subject is constituted extimately because it is not entirely discontinuous with what is outside of it (such as, for example, images, the Other, language) and what is outside can therefore also be highly intimate. This is what Rothenberg, following Lacan, calls a 'Möbius subject'; like the Möbius strip – a circle of ribbon twisted and joined at both ends, now with only one surface – there are distinct locations but no absolute separation from inside and outside. Never wholly sealed off from its outside, the Möbius subject perpetually exceeds precise determination or enclosure by its imaginary and symbolic registers, such that what is ostensibly outside is experienced as intimately present (Rothenberg, 2010: 30–45). Thus, for Lacan, the unconscious operates outside the subject, in the world it inhabits and not discretely contained in the space of the mind. So, for example, flags, memorials, photographs or rhetoric are all ostensibly external objects or practices that frequently evoke something deeply intimate to the subject. Intense feelings are transferred on to them and experienced as emanating independently from their own objective qualities (see Kingsbury, 2007).

The situational exigence is thus an extimate cause in that empirical events come to be ascribed a status of profound and intimate significance, setting in motion the subject's desire by naming a defect in need of resolution. As an empirical disruption or blockage, the exigence is identified as the traumatic source of the subject's failure fully to realise its desire. Of course, the subject already exceeds its symbolic mandate and can never be satisfied. But the exigence offers an opportunity to objectify excess via an external event that then allocates responsibility for unachieved desire onto something concrete that stands for its own excessiveness to itself. That way, the possibility of realising desire is held open and the situation is transformed into an opportunity to reactivate the subject as desiring (that is, seeking satisfaction). Following the logic noted in the previous section, we can conceive the rhetorical situation as the process in which an exigence that may initially generate intense anxiety (such as excessive and traumatic violence), presenting its disruption in the form of the Thing, subsequently being transformed by rhetorical mediation into a manifestation of the *objet petit a* (such as an urge to 'give service' in a time of national peril). That is, by way of effective rhetorical action, the exigence is symbolised, no longer as an overwhelming traumatic presence but as the marker of the missing object of desire that the subject longed for all along. The exigence opens a space for fantasising wherein the disruption brought by the real to the symbolic order is refigured as the revelation of some missing quality.

What is important to note here is that the exigence is not a discrete event with positive, objective qualities, as Bitzer initially implies. It tears a hole in our symbolic fabric and acts as an uncanny object that defies sense. It is not a definable entity so much as a negation, a gap in our ability to define anything. For that reason, it can take on vast, frightening proportions until we find ways to assimilate it, or symbolise it. That way, we set its parameters and organise our desire around it. But what causes the demand for rhetoric is therefore not a positive force wholly outside the subject so much as an irruption of the real within our intimately-held symbolic space that is then objectified in such a way that we can fold it back into a narrative or argument.

An example of this kind of extreme situation is the terrorist attack on the US on 11 September 2001. The immediate event and aftermath of the attack was a moment of utter shock and disorientation. The extent of the assault, the scale of death and devastation it brought, and the origins of the attackers and their plans was not known and therefore could not be quickly registered in the way, say, minor incidents are. But as the immediate causes and consequences came into view, it became possible to react rhetorically (and politically; soon militarily) both in the media and in government. Reaction involved assembling a new symbolic frame that not only described what had happened but, moreover, how it was to be understood. That way, the rhetoric of media commentators and politicians could find a way not only to position the audience (as observers and victims of a devastating incident brought by terrorists) but also to cast that position in a light that would enable them to feel and experience themselves as protagonists in an intelligible, global drama. That is to say, the rhetoric that followed managed to coordinate the desires of citizens by presenting them in the form of a 'melodrama', that is, as innocent victims of a monstrous evil, thereby channelling the incalculable excess of feeling brought by the attacks into an attitude of righteous anger directed at the jihadist enemies of the US (see Anker, 2014). For psychoanalytic commentators such as Todd McGowan, this powerfully dramatic reaction enabled citizens to 'enjoy' their situation by permitting them to subscribe to a narrative of loss (McGowan, 2013: 159–61). Although ordinary Americans were in evident and genuine pain and suffering, repeated acts of solidarity and narratives of malign intent by people 'envious' of the US's success, helped reposition their attitudes by disposing them to their situation anew: namely, as being at war against a new enemy. The initial trauma of the attacks was thus transformed into a focused hostility built around a fantasy combing sacrifice, loss, and vengeance.

Visualising the Political Stain

I have argued that an excess in subjectivity is central to rhetorical practice in so far as it urges subjects to 'see things anew', to frame arguments through fantasies, and thus to intervene in rhetorical situations. Rhetoric's task is often to excite and coordinate desire by appealing to this excess, figuring desire as objectively caused, and coordinating arguments around an actual or anticipated sense of traumatic loss. What is important to underline here is that excess prevents subjects from subscribing fully to a symbolic register. We never really know what the Other wants and so we never really know what it wants from us. Excess stands simultaneously for an opacity in the symbolic order and in ourselves. This opacity frequently confounds public speech and debate – what, we constantly ask, do politicians *really* mean when they say x or y? And do they really say what they mean? – yet it is precisely the failure of symbolic closure that holds open the possibility of re-appropriating public discourse, supplying an answer to what it is politicians do want (our money, their own rewards, ideological control and so on). By consequence, in political life, our attention is never simply on what is directly before us but, more importantly, what it is that we *can't find* in it. To participate rhetorically in politics is not just to have a preferred 'vision' of the world and pursue it (such as when one subscribes to a political ideology) but to be ineluctably pulled into the gaps and cracks that open up in the surfaces of society and draw us to question its symbolic demands. Political discourse is at its most rhetorically inventive when it directs us to these gaps on our horizons, the blank spots that distort our vision and, thereby, provoke our desire.

One way of thinking about the uncanny visuality of political discourse and the place of rhetoric in it is by way of the idea of 'the gaze'. The gaze has been widely used to describe the way a certain direction of sight, or look, dominates a particular field. Feminists have highlighted the 'male gaze' to understand how a preferred way of viewing women as objects of desire dominates in patriarchal society. A similar notion was employed in 1970s film theory (which often drew upon feminist interventions) to explain how films tell us stories from unquestioned narrative perspectives that present men as protagonists and women as mere love interests (see Boothby, 2001: 252–5). Lacan's idea of the gaze, however, is rather different since it is not about the subject's mastery over what it sees but, rather, about its submission. For Lacan, who builds on the later philosophy of Merleau-Ponty, the gaze describes not a subject's point of view but, rather, something that seems to be *looking at the subject*. It denotes a presence in the 'scopic field' that looks back at the viewer without being visible itself. It is not about what we actually see, but what we can't see in what we look at. The gaze is thus an indiscernible visual 'lure' that, like the Thing discussed above, captivates the subject and generates anxiety. For Lacan, it is another manifestation of the *objet a*, an indeterminate presence (or lack) that cannot be precisely located but which, nonetheless, captures the viewer's attention. It functions, he says, like a 'stain' that disrupts the otherwise smooth homogeneity of a surface (1977: 74). As a stain, or visual distortion, it encourages the subject to imagine there is something hidden beneath a symbolic surface that explains the Other's enjoyment. The gaze thus describes not the subject's desire as it seeks mastery over its object (as in the male gaze) but 'the underside of consciousness', that which activates the subject's desire by figuring a locus of absence (1977: 83).

In Lacanian film theory, for example, the gaze concerns not what is actually seen in a movie but what cannot be seen so that, by virtue of its very absence, our investment in the film is sustained (see McGowan, 2007). Movies are typically organised around a disruption in the field of vision that ensures that the symbolic aspects of the film – the characters, dialogue and narrative – are constantly moving around an unknown element, which keeps spectators watching. The filmic gaze is thus a visual distortion deployed to incite and sustain the viewers' desire. That distortion is sometimes given a degree of presence as, for example, a monster that cannot be properly seen, an unknown thief or killer who evades capture, or a motive that cannot be grasped. Of course, most mainstream movies eventually aim to resolve the discomfort brought by the gaze by revealing the monster, the murderer, or the motive. This is achieved by finally uncovering the ultimate object of desire that reveals the source of enjoyment (destroying the earth, stealing in order to gain untold riches, or demonstrating a hidden love, for example). In such instances, the previously unknown object is revealed as a specific, knowable thing and the symbolic order is thereby restored, usually to great acclaim – and desire subsequently dissipates.

This is how filmic fantasy tends to operate in cinema: by deploying uncertainty around an absence in our field of vision (despite everything we actually see) and then, eventually, resolving our anxiety by revealing the true source of the Other's enjoyment. The gaps in the symbolic order are thereby momentarily mended by revealing the stain to be merely a contingent (rather than permanent) disruption.

Lacanian film theory demonstrates how the *objet a* operates as a blank spot in the visual field that nonetheless grips the subject by separating it off, if only temporarily, from its adherence to the symbolic order. Our expectations of a law-enforcing hero (for example) is held off while we are left to figure out what are his real motives (eg his enduring love for his family, his commitment to justice, his sheer arrogant will power). While fantasy scenarios eventually aim to reconcile viewers to the symbolic order by plot resolutions that restore social and moral principles, they do so only by virtue of an initial distortion that opens in the subject a disjuncture with the symbolic order. What is important here is the point that films only work because they recruit the desire of the viewer. The gaze is the mechanism that, by making the viewer uncertain about what the Other wants, reattaches subjects to the symbolic order by stoking their desire to know the source of its enjoyment.

The psychopolitics of film, I want to suggest, is also what is at work in many speech situations. In some ways, speeches function like mini-movies by setting out visual narratives through which audiences are encouraged not only to see the world but, moreover, to narrate their role in it. Public speeches frequently supply imagistic stories that highlight a political stain distorting the field and so exciting the audience's interest. In this way, the audience's desire is integral to the argument, which acts like a summons to its unconscious urge to know what the Other enjoys. For example, President John F Kennedy's famous Inaugural speech of 1961 depicted a Cold War international landscape divided by ideology to which he made repeated appeals ('Let both sides ...') for cooperation to replace hostility (see Kennedy, 1999). Oscillating between contrasting images of 'hope' and 'the dark powers of destruction' exemplified by political enmity and military confrontation, the stain was manifest as a disabling uncertainty, an anxiety-inducing absence about how opposed worldviews might co-exist. The resolution offered, however, was not any specific policy but, rather, a challenge to American citizens *themselves* to rethink their priorities and adopt the 'energy, the faith, the devotion' of a 'new generation'. What the Other (the international order) truly enjoys, he implies, is seeing held aloft the beacon of 'light' (emanating from the American character) that heralds a new sense of common endeavour. This light (the 'torch' passed to the new generation) is, tellingly, the means to see and not merely something to be seen.

A very different tone is given in President Trump's Inaugural of 2017 (see Trump, 2017). But it is no less an effort to invoke the presence of a stain on the political horizon and thereby to arouse public desire. Trump launches straight in to an antithesis between 'the establishment' who have indulged their careers and the 'citizens' who have endured suffering. He points explicitly to urban poverty and crime, job losses, and failing educational systems – all visible symptoms of decline in what, notoriously, he describes as an 'American carnage', invoking social destruction and bodily dismemberment: 'Politicians prospered – but the jobs left and the factories closed'. This imagery of a hollowed-out society and of establishment neglect then invites acclaim for his principle of 'America First', a resetting of priorities that promises to 'bring back' jobs, business, infrastructure and, ultimately, 'a new national pride'. Trump's address is undoubtedly less artful than Kennedy's and lacks his rousing appeal to a higher sense of purpose. But then, that was his point. The stain is here the self-serving sophistry of a political class who cannot stop talking of higher purposes. What it reveals is the establishment enjoying itself at everyone else's expense. The remedy is therefore more transactional than spiritually challenging – it is to return to the citizens the basic enjoyment they have lost, which comes in his final flourish listing American strength, pride, wealth and security. These are imaginary qualities, not for lighting the way for others to follow as in Kennedy's speech, but what Americans perceive as their basic entitlements. If JFK's speech invited its audience to imagine itself as a heroic generation charged with leading the world in a time of darkness, Trump's invites his audience simply to see themselves get what they're owed.

Conclusion

In this chapter we have in fact returned to the question (raised initially in Chapter 1) of how speech and rhetoric relate to the perceptual and emotional capacities of the body. I have argued that Lacan's reworking of psychoanalysis offers a framework to understand how rhetoric manages the excess of subjective desire over its imaginary and symbolic formation. The central contribution of Lacan's theory of discourse is his formulation of fantasy, conceived not as a make-believe world but as a way to invest desire in the enigma of a lost enjoyment. Fantasy is thus a way to dispose us towards reality and thereby direct our reason. By transforming subjective anxiety in the face of the Thing into an image of potential fulfilment, it acts as a stimulus to desire and permits the subject a degree of safe enjoyment. Political speech and argument therefore take their cue from concrete situations whose varying disruptions to the symbolic order enable anxieties to be rhetorically refashioned. The work of rhetoric can thus be understood as something like that of a movie, namely to draw attention to a stain in the visual field that summons us to question what the Other enjoys. That way rhetoric works not just on our minds but on deeper, corporeal reservoirs of desire so as to encourage us to see the world anew.

4. The Force of the Bitter Argument

Few habits reveal the vibrant connection between speech and bodily passions better than insults and verbal abuse. Malicious remarks, derogatory comments, personal abuse, demonising attitudes, cruel, spiteful and objectifying language, and general misanthropic hostility all mobilise intense corporeal forces against perceived adversaries, usually so as to refuse any obligation to hear them. More often than not, such remarks are themselves directed at the bodies of those they aim to disqualify, marking them out as undeserving of serious engagement or respectful treatment. It is common to dismiss this type of speech as illegitimate and unfitting for rational attention. Rhetorically speaking, hostile and *ad hominem* remarks are typically registered as 'fallacies', which one scholar of logic rightfully describes as 'the death of argument', since they disrupt the elaboration of discursive exchange by effectively collapsing debate (Woods, 2004).

But even though vituperation – or what I have called 'the force of the bitter argument' – frequently steps beyond the acceptable limits of reasoned dialogue, it remains one of the most common aspects of public and political speech. Although we rarely celebrate this antagonistic dimension as a model of human communication, it is perpetually present as the underside to most social and political discourse. If it appears as the death of argument, it is nonetheless a death to which we find ourselves repeatedly returning – and usually not without a visible degree of relish. Far from nobly committing themselves to the force of 'the better argument', as Habermas puts it of his 'ideal speech situation' (1996a: 103), political actors are regularly inclined to be contemptuous of their adversaries and often keen to diminish them and the cases they make. While this does not always lead to outright confrontation, nonetheless there is what Chantal Mouffe calls 'an ever-present propensity for violence' in public discourse that is too readily occluded by the idealisation of deliberation (see Mouffe, 2000).

The repeated return of this death drive to argument is a reminder that controversial discourse involves a struggle to figure the space of argument itself, sometimes by dramatically shifting the boundaries of attention and thereby our evaluation of the objects within them. Vituperation, in its many, varied and often inventive forms, can be a powerfully effective means to reassert control over discursive interaction, perhaps by simply disrupting discourse or distracting attention but also by polarising the field, presenting alternative positions to one's own as bearers of an unacceptable stain. Cruel and hostile remarks typically gravitate towards the hyperbolic, exaggerating the horror of alternative opinions to disable serious engagement with them, and usually drawing attention to a purportedly excessive enjoyment by the adversary. It is no surprise, then, that at their most extreme invective and hateful remarks radically reduce the opponent's motivations to sexual pleasures, obscene and perverse bodily gratifications (or just body parts), or label them simply as objects of disgust. Far from being a marginal practice, however, speech of this type reveals the underlying pressure of the real beneath our imaginary and symbolic investments, threatening to destabilise them.

Below, I explore the psychopolitics of vituperation and hateful speech by drawing upon Lacan's ideas, elaborated in earlier chapters, regarding the tension between symbolic and imaginary registers. I begin by looking generally at the relationship between speech, violence and the logic of sacrifice. Politics is often understood to involve a rejection of violence, but I suggest it is better to conceive it as the sublimation of potentially violent confrontation. Because the full enjoyment of desire must be sacrificed for the sake of security and co-operation via the Other, politics typically entails a managed form of conflict, rubbing up against the boundaries and limits of shared identity. Argumentative controversies therefore testify to the, sometimes explosive, tensions and misalignments between images of personal and collective identity and the symbolic exchanges actors engage in so as to preserve and advance themselves alongside others. Political actors are persistently under pressure to defend, adjust, or even recompose the images to which they subscribe to enable them to co-exist or even cooperate with rivals. This tension between imaginary egos and the symbolic terms of their interaction plays out in public rhetoric as individuals struggle to resist and control each other's manoeuvres. Vituperation of some kind, then, is an unavoidable feature of this type of sublimated conflict among adversaries who regard each other as rivals for influence and power.

Yet not all rivalry can be contained within the terms of an assumed sacrifice of enjoyment. Hateful speech and behaviour emerge at the point that a shared symbolic space breaks down. As the recent controversy over left antisemitism in the British Labour Party reveals, investments of desire in imaginary constructs can intensify and a form of paranoid hostility emerges that brooks little or no symbolic mediation. In that scenario, political rhetoric functions to exclude and vilify the other for an excessive, destructive enjoyment – an intense, surplus satisfaction beyond mere pleasure – perceived to be taken at one's expense. In the case of Labour, a rhetorical hostility to Israel (rather than Jews as such) emerged as the vehicle for a hateful politics that affirms radical left identity, yet at the cost of conciliation with its antagonists. If hatefulness is to be productive rather than simply destructive, I suggest at the end, it would help to learn lessons from other rhetorical genres in which conciliation rather than expulsion is prized.

Speech, Violence, and the Logic of Sacrifice

We sometimes think of speech as a largely mundane 'civic' practice of communicative exchange designed to accomplish the practical tasks of politics and government. But public discourse regularly magnifies antagonisms that are often absent in the routine exchanges of everyday talk. Although political discourse is frequently idealised as conforming to a pragmatic and peaceable model of human sociability, this is usually at the expense of giving recognition to the aggressive, competitive and persistently malicious undercurrents that circulate around and inflect public deliberations (see Saint-Amand, 1996).

We might better understand political speech and language as *sublimations* of violence; the displacement onto formalised, ritual exchanges of an otherwise ready propensity to aggressive, destructive and antisocial behaviour. The regular incivility of Prime Minister's Questions in the UK legislature, for example, expresses in stylized form a hostile division between two opposed sides of the House of Commons. Although many legislatures are replete with arcane conventions and ritualised practices that make them seem harmless, even quaint, chambers of debate can be raucous, hostile and profoundly uncivil environments. Not unreasonably, of course, political discourse is widely imagined to be the very opposite of physical violence. In key respects, that is true: to talk is not to engage directly in wanton destruction of people and property; life is preserved, and conflicts may be resolved through dialogue and compromise. But speech is not the pure antonym of violent behaviour; destructive conflict remains an ever-present possibility (especially if resolutions to disputes are not found) and, frequently, speech itself stokes violence or tries to make us complicit with it. So, if we set aside the tendency to moralise speech and, instead, think of language as the sublimation of violence and enmity – that is, the transformation of the capacity for brute force into another form, rather than its total negation – it becomes clearer why insulting and vituperative rhetoric might be of interest.

For rhetoricians, public speech usually entails taking sides, making and defending contentious claims by appealing to arguments and evidence, minimising the strengths of opposing views and neutralising logical or ethical inconsistencies, sometimes (but not always) in order to promote a shared judgement or orientation. Argument is a highly motivated form of speech and subsists in the realm of controversy where disagreement and conflict characterise human relations (see Fish, 2016). Speech is, often, the medium of violence's sublimation into a regulated and managed form of conflict. In that respect, underlying all political discourse is the re-enactment of a distinctly *sacrificial* logic. Opposed images of social order are exposed to each other so that through their mutual clash a symbolic principle of exchange is ultimately reaffirmed. The prospect that any one individual, group or party might have full freedom to exercise their own preferred vision of social arrangements is sacrificed for rules that delimit their autonomy and make politics a locus of competing desires rather than brute force. Public debates and controversies are undergirded by an implicit awareness of the prospect of damaging violence and the necessity of mutual sacrifice, which transforms, or sublimates, this possibility into largely symbolic exchanges (see McAfee, 2008).

Political cultures are therefore characterised by discursive conflicts that frequently resemble, or are redescribed in terms of, forms of combat or physical confrontation. Verbal 'sparring', words as 'weapons', 'fighting a war of words', verbal 'assault' and so forth are all phrases that conjure images of competitive sport or war. While direct violence is, almost uniformly, explicitly looked upon with disdain, there can be a considerable amount of leeway given to adversaries in political dispute so long as they refrain from physical harm. Dismissive attitudes; accusations of impropriety, hypocrisy, falsehood, and criminality; personal insults and attacks on individual associations – these are all common outside (and occasionally inside) debating chambers. Which is why many parliaments have specific prohibitions in their rules of conduct to prevent the most hostile and demeaning forms of spoken attack. In some political cultures, personal insults and disrespectful epithets are common, while others have strong guidelines to prevent debaters reducing public argument to interpersonal abuse. Public language therefore offers a means to censure, demean or ridicule opponents and, thereby, diminish their credibility to the public. Although actual fighting does on occasion break out in parliaments and in public arenas among politicians, hostile forms of speech typically transfer direct force into a symbolic arena where the outcome is only one of looking foolish or losing the respect of one's peers. Opposed arguments are then represented as alternate individual points of view, with the esteem of others serving as the ultimate determinant of success.

In classical rhetoric, it was not uncommon to hear the rhetoric of invective *(vituperiato)* at work and it was a regular theme in rhetorical handbooks. Cicero himself was a highly able mobiliser of vitriol and insult (see Conley, 2010: 31–40). Highlighting the personal failings of an individual politician, the associations he made, or his misjudgements was understood to be a legitimate means to apportion blame, polarise argument and so clarify the differences at stake in a dispute. Revealing the personal limitations of an opponent made it possible to render one's own argument plausible and, it was hoped, preferable over the alternative. While often looked upon with disdain, *ad hominem* arguments, which are directed at the individual and not the argument, aim to mobilise shame, sometimes by implying guilt by association with misdeeds or disreputable people and actions. Thomas Conley lists a number of the most frequent topics of Roman invective, which include: embarrassing family origin, physical appearance, gluttony and drunkenness, hypocrisy, unacceptable sexual conduct, aspirations to tyranny, and oratorical ineptitude (see 2010: 37–8). Although these may seem absurd or trivial, diminishing the status and reputation of a rival afforded a foothold for enhancing one's own. In an elite environment where public recognition mattered highly, deploying invective to insult one's opponent and thereby attack his argument was a serviceable device that revealed the intelligence of a speaker. In such circumstances, words can be destructive and if careers depend on the maintenance of the high regard of others, vituperation threatens to be profoundly harmful.

What, then, might Lacan's insights tell us about rivalry in political rhetoric? There are three things worth noting, which build upon the discussion in previous chapters of the interactions of imaginary, symbolic and real registers of subjectivity. First, although political speech is employed by politicians to enhance their own personal status and success, it is not exclusively defensive of individual egos, social interests or personalities. Certainly, political actors speak to images of collective identity and purpose, projected as though already unified and robust positions. But, as Lacan pointed out, if subjectivity is reduced to a closed gestalt – that is, if actors address each other only from their imaginary identifications – the result would be paranoia, permanent rivalry and aggression. Social relations would collapse into 'a permanent "it's you or me" form of war' where discourse forms 'the retorting aggressiveness of verbal echo' (Lacan, 2006: 356). While this verbal echo is undoubtedly familiar in politics, formal debate enables the displacement of outright hostile confrontation by partially exposing imaginary identities to the shifting surfaces of signifiers. There isn't just 'us' and 'them' but a shared relation to the Other: the master signifiers of the law, national interest, the common good, justice, mutual respect, and so on, support symbolic exchange, often in a lively discordance. Actual physical confrontation is reduced in favour of verbal 'sparring' – 'antagonists' become 'adversaries' as Mouffe puts it (2000: 102–3) – when erstwhile enemies come to relate not as self-contained or pre-constituted unities but as relatively persuadable rivals by way of the signifiers that mediate their interactions. Political discourse is often controversial and discomforting precisely because speakers are perpetually exposed to the potential deconstruction of their identities, pressuring each other to accede to demands and desires they initially refuse.

Second, if political rivalry entails the relatively orderly assault on imaginary unities primarily through symbolic manoeuvres, inevitably that involves the mediation of conflict by rhetoric and rhetorical strategies. To speak, 'speak out', interrogate, question, petition, ridicule and so on, are all rhetorical choices to engage in the symbolic re-contexualisation and re-elaboration of discursive stances. Claims by one side to have a common interest at heart, for example, are exposed to rigorous questioning and revision by opponents seeking to test and reveal unacknowledged fixations or commitments folded into one's preferred self-image. To argue politically is usually to refigure one's adversary and their programmes, ideas, and goals in ways that disrupt or even destroy their cherished identifications and, thereby, foreground one's own. Functioning within the constraints of a sacrificial logic, adversaries use each others' statements and actions to expose contradictions or inconsistencies, and so reveal an inability to meet the demands of the Other. Of course, such disruptions can, in principle, go on forever without conclusion. The repetitive to-and-fro of political dispute can frequently seem tedious and ritualised, undertaken simply for the sake of refusing any advantage to the adversary. Which is why most formalised arenas of debate and disputation are inclined to arbitrary closure that bring verbal conflict to an end (though, of course, they continue unofficially): elections, referendums, timed debates, news cycles and so on all supply constraining endpoints to delimit rhetorical controversy. Equally, rules of debate, censorship, and the simple refusal to acknowledge or speak with rivals also reduce the potential damage of ongoing symbolic conflict (see Palonen, 2019).

Third, vital to the experience of rhetorical controversy are irruptions of enjoyment as symbolic interactions disrupt rival imaginary identifications. There is, for example, an intense satisfaction in revealing one's adversary as an inconsistent reasoner, a hypocrite, or delusional dreamer indulging in self-serving sophistry. The opportunity in public debates to re-punctuate another's symbolic chains resembles the way Freud explained jokes: speakers extend or reorder the other's words and arguments in ways that are surprising and unexpected, introducing unintended conclusions that sabotage the assumed integrity of one's interlocutor (see McGowan, 2013: 76–78). Much of the immediate thrill of argumentative controversy stems from the excitement of deflating an opponent's irritating self-regard. In 2012, then Australian Prime Minister, Julia Gillard, took an opportunity in Parliament to denounce the opposition leader, Tony Abbott, for his persistent sexism and misogyny. 'The Leader of the Opposition says that people who hold sexist views and who are misogynists are not appropriate for high office. Well I hope the Leader of the Opposition has got a piece of paper and he is writing out his resignation. Because if he wants to know what misogyny looks like in modern Australia, he doesn't need a motion in the House of Representatives, he needs a mirror' (Gillard, 2012). Gillard then proceeded to repeat numerous statements by Abbott, turning his own words against him to expose his own vulgarity and hypocrisy. The speech became briefly notorious not least for its bitingly effective spearing of Abbott's pomposity.

But enjoyment is not limited simply to the sabotage of the other's self-image. The elaboration of arguments involves articulating pathways – interlinking signifiers – the effect of which is, moreover, to capture a force beyond speech that guarantees the speaker's or the speech's authenticity and restraint. In this instance, it is less an enjoyment experienced and more an enjoyment *sacrificed* that gives rhetoric its underlying attraction (see McGowan, 2013). Political speakers regularly appeal to tragic events or experiences that invoke the presence of an overwhelming loss or sense of limit that exceeds description but which, nonetheless, propels their own speech and roots it in a plenitude of bodily sensation. This is the figuration of sacrifice, the invocation of a violence that constantly resets political discourse around a new polarity. Governments and oppositions are forever inviting us to think that we are on the cusp of societal collapse brought, invariably, by catastrophic policy choices, emergent threats, and weak leaders. It would be wrong, then, to think that the sacrifice of violence for peaceful discourse is a completed act in the past, a situation in history from which we cannot remove ourselves and that now imposes permanent prohibitions on what we can say or do. Lacan's work suggests that the logic of sacrifice is something that is constantly repeated and therefore we cannot ever be sanguine about living inside an established consensus where we know for sure what the Other wants.

So what is sacrifice? Psychoanalytic thinkers, among others, have long been drawn to the notion of sacrifice because it describes both a social and psychical practice by which violence is incorporated into the social field as loss (see Boothby, 2001: 175–89; Recalcati, 2017; Eagleton, 2018). Socially, sacrifice is a ritual that involves giving up some surplus of communal wealth to a deity or a sacred object of veneration in order to ensure that the community is bound together symbolically.

As Boothby understands it, sacrificial objects – animals, persons, or merely food – are a means to re-enact socially the process of castration, that is, of psychically surrendering some object of brute existence in order affirm a higher principle of the social order (2001: 185). In this, sacrifice concretely performs the action of the death drive. It projects onto a wider stage the subject's relinquishing its intense attachment to the mother figure in the process of taking up the symbolic mandate by which it enters adult society. The renunciation of organic bodily integrity so as to register with a system of signification is mirrored in the social ritual of killing and dismembering animals or surrendering food in order to institute a symbolic exchange in which complex human needs are coordinated and coherently managed. The symbolic order of mediated exchange replaces the order of organic objects just as, for Lacan, the infant's incestuous enjoyment is sacrificed for a symbolic role ruled by the signifier. To exist without such sacrifice, underscores Recalcati (2017: 24), is, like madness and perversion, the 'mirage of an enjoyment free from loss and desire'.

In Boothby's account, sacrifice establishes the social bond as such by incorporating the real into social existence (2001: 185). Sacrifice creates the very possibility of a system of relations that makes society possible, just as in Lacan's account it makes subjectivity possible by enabling the ego to negotiate difference. But sacrifice is an ambivalent process: it is both destructive *and* creative at the same time, violating imaginary integrity as well as installing order around the centrality of the Other (Boothby, 2001: 187). The peculiar rites and strict prohibitions surrounding most sacrificial practices enact this shift from an organic way of living to a system of exchange that enables regular and complex interactions. In McGowan's view, this logic remains fundamental to society because sacrifice, both in the form of rituals and as a principle itself, 'offers an opportunity for returning to the point at which the social order constituted itself' (2013: 147). Sacrifice is repeated socially and drawn back to memory – in the form of war memorial services, for example – as a way to return to the founding loss of society. What is achieved by the repetition of sacrificial memory is a justification for the loss of enjoyment and the urgency for prohibition via symbolic laws. In so doing, the principle of sacrifice accentuates the investment in loss as the basis of society. What is held in common is therefore something absent. It is not a positive object but, rather, a non-object. It is precisely the traumatic loss instantiated in the act of sacrifice that, as Georges Batailles argues, is itself deeply enjoyable (see Webb, 1993: 59–87). Although modern society differs from pre-modern society in that it tends to disavow openly validating sacrifice, re-enacting and remembering sacrifice continues to be socially significant because it returns subjects to an enjoyable experience of loss that brings to the fore a shared symbolic debt.

Far from being a one-off event, sacrifice is something that society ends up repeating discursively in order to re-imagine and thereby reinforce, or refigure, the constitution of society by invoking its traumatic origins. Although collective sacrificial acts are made, for the most part, only in wars or moments of disaster, where loss of life occurs, the logic of sacrifice nonetheless persists in contemporary cultures. Because of its socially unifying effect, images of founding conflicts persist, especially in nationalistic ideologies which often point to a sacrificial moment, whether real or mythical, as part of a narrative of origins or new beginnings. For example, the Second World War, and particularly the experience of air attack by the Nazis, is a powerful, sacrificial memory in post-war British political discourse. An imagined sense of having witnessed the 'end of the world' (Lowe, 2017) came to underscore a variety of political programmes and rhetorical strategies: conservatives reference it as a marker of British character, while radicals underscore its production of a new consensus around state intervention in welfare provision. But what is unifying here is not a positive principle of the good (on which there are clear differences of opinion) but a shared enjoyment of loss that each side tries to monopolise with its own narrative.

So how does this relate to vituperative rhetoric? The kinds of sharp disagreement that produces abusive exchanges and insulting behaviour testifies to the way a shared symbolic bond forces speakers to sublimate their hostility as robust exchanges. Because the Other never reveals what it wants, adversaries struggle to define the loss that unifies us. Disagreement over a common and unifying loss raises the constant prospect, on all sides, that the adversary is enjoying or endorsing illicit enjoyment. In such circumstances, transgressions of formal, and very often informal, symbolic principles open up the demand for a gesture of censure, for example, so as to reaffirm the primacy of the unifying principle. Personal insults and vitriol, I want to suggest, impatiently gesture towards this sacrificial mode, typically by ascribing a secret enjoyment indulged by the transgressor (or by the transgressor against the 'establishment') and thus a refusal to accept the condition of loss. Of course, such censure works at a number of different layers: politicians, commentators and activists persistently call each other out for inappropriate choices (of words, beliefs, clothes, or friendships), unfounded claims, or just behaviours that are deemed 'shameful' to some degree: accusations of sexual impropriety, betrayal, corruption and venality, and so on. Think, for example, of the brief furore over President Trump's remark that there was 'blame on both sides' in the clashes in August 2017 between neo-Nazis and anti-racist protesters in Charlottesville, Virginia, where one protester was killed. Trump's repeated refusal to allocate responsibility specifically to white supremacists appeared to draw 'moral equivalency' between all sides of that conflict. This diminished the assumed salience of an anti-racist consensus – a refusal to let racists legitimately enjoy their prejudices – and earned the President public censure from across the political spectrum (see Sheer and Haberman, 2017).

Shaming is indeed one of the most common critical rhetorical gestures in domestic political discourse because it invokes the wider community of auditors to view the transgressing speaker(s) as operating on the margins of established symbolic space, highlighting a stain to be removed. As Gillard continued in her speech: 'what the Leader of the Opposition should be ashamed of is his performance in this Parliament and the sexism he brings with it'. By invoking shame, the critic implies that the Other might yet exert a disciplining force, if not on the transgressors then at least on those who may be inclined to support them. In turn, those who are censured by insult and invective may complain of undue restrictions being placed on their discourse. 'Honest' opinion, they opine, is being closed down by overbearing 'political correctness', voices are rendered 'silent' by those who refuse to hear genuine criticism, purposefully misunderstand their point, and so on. A surprisingly large amount of public discourse, especially in the mass media, is taken up with this combined resisting and policing of speech around accusations, for example of racism, sexism, excessive vulgarity or plain rudeness.

I have claimed that political speech functions to sublimate violence, rather than wholly eliminate it. Because, as Lacan suggests, subjectivity is itself a site of intrinsic conflict and controversy – revealed in tensions between imaginary and symbolic registers – political discourse aims to control this otherwise unstable clash of desires. This is achieved largely by argumentative contests between adversaries that attack and diminish rival imaginary identities and attachments, as well as advance their own. If such contests operate primarily on a symbolic plane – they are mostly undertaken in speech and language by means of signifiers – nonetheless they can be experienced, at least intermittently, as deeply personal and collective conflicts of an affective kind. Rhetorical contests can thus be said to help shift the potential for imaginary violence onto a more orderly and peaceable – but no less hostile – symbolic stage. As a consequence, the threat of the real to imaginary identity is rhetorically refigured around the loss or sacrifice of enjoyment. It is on this basis, I continue below, that we might also comprehend the psychopolitics of 'hate speech'.

Rhetorics of Hate

If formal democratic debate and advocacy is undertaken in a structured and relatively civil manner, nonetheless, I have suggested that, by their very nature, partisan conflicts and political disagreements at times give rise to fairly uncivil conduct (see Herbst, 2010). Accusations of 'hateful' behaviour abound in civil and political dispute, often where entrenched and deeply opposed positions are taken, which invest heavily in imaginary identification and are unable to find symbolic mediation. Hate, then, might be understood to encapsulate – broadly speaking – an appraisal of group and personal dispositions where such mediation is refused or unavailable. In that case, far from being exceptional, the appearance of hateful speech and conduct is a common recurrence and ever-present possibility in diverse and plural societies. But hate can also erupt as an antagonism that is so hostile it escapes the logic of sacrifice altogether. In such situations, hateful speech and behaviour is no longer a form of censure but, instead, a mode of enjoyment itself.

Of course, what counts as 'hate speech' – or as sufficiently hateful speech to demand action by authorities – varies greatly in time and place and is thus open to interpretation. That is why it can be so difficult to regulate in law. We may be able to distinguish direct solicitations to violence with some precision, but it is harder to defend penalising *all* hateful opinions (for a discussion, see Heinze, 2013; Waldron, 2012). Malicious comments, disrespectful and unpleasant remarks about the integrity of other opinions, peoples, their bodies, customs or actions are a routine, if somewhat distasteful, part of cultural and political life, just like invective. Scorn, denigration, slurs, expressions of contempt, or use of hostile and reductive epithets are unwholesome but nevertheless common enough accompaniments to civil discourse in as much as, at the very least, they mark out the limits of symbolic exchange and reveal fundamental clashes over shared priorities. While insulting remarks sometimes escalate into wider conflicts (see Korostelina, 2014), what is important to gauge is not merely the presence of particular words or phrases but the intersubjective relations that they figure (see Waltman and Haas, 2011).

Clearly, 'hate' covers an enormous spectrum of formulations in speech, making it unclear precisely *where* the hate is manifest in specific utterances: is it in the use of specific words and ideas to describe others? Or in the tone and force used to demean them? Perhaps, maybe, in the atmospheres and feelings these leave behind? Hateful things may be said with little intention to hurt, or with an abundance of intention but to little or no effect. Vernacular vocabularies are replete with unacknowledged terms of abuse – particularly about women, non-heterosexuals, people of colour, and foreigners – such that they can be employed as if they bore no offence at all. Hateful motivation is often coupled with other affective states that enhance or obscure it, such as intense feelings of affection or extreme aggression and rage. The degrees of hate's intensity, duration and discursive organisation can vary considerably and, undoubtedly, the cultural and political context will make a difference to how it is perceived and experienced (see Boromisza-Habashi, 2013). But hate – rather than plain hostility or anger, which may present themselves merely as 'vehement' opinions – usually threatens to disrupt the symbolic organisation of discourse by dissolving the boundaries and distinctions that separate off public opinions from merely privately-held beliefs. When we hate in public, we don't just hold strong opinions about a matter (a person, situation, or issue); we refuse the very space that matter occupies in public discourse. Which is why hating can amount to a wholesale refusal to tolerate the presence of something or to respect the personal boundaries of the other, paradoxically by dwelling on the other's very existence. In these circumstances, expressions of hate may be incitations to intolerance and even physical violence. It is therefore worth being attentive to the way that hate unfolds rhetorically in particular situations and in different kinds of argumentative framework.

What psychoanalytical enquiry alerts us to is the way hate reveals something structural within subjectivity that plays out as an intense hostility towards others: namely, the defensive character of the ego. Hateful remarks and behaviours fend off or expel intolerable feelings that threaten the integrity of the imaginary self. This is not simply an expulsion of displeasurable sensations – according to the logic of Freud's pleasure principle – but a deeper existential encounter. As we have seen, according to Lacan the imaginary ego is an intrinsically defensive site of investment, prone to aggressive and rivalrous encounters with the other egos that threaten its illusory unity. Unlike mere frustration at displeasurable sensations, narcissistic rivalry takes on a more obsessive and paranoid character, singling out an enemy and dwelling upon images of the other's invasive presence. The other is, or has, something the narcissistic ego wants, and the contest unravels as a confusing oscillation between desire and repulsion. As Lacan suggests, this 'narcissistic aggressiveness' is effectively captured in Melanie Klein's account of 'envy', whereby the infant attacks its object as a defence against a perceived (or anticipated) incursion into its own integrity (Lacan, 2006: 93–5. See also Klein, 1997; Klein and Riviere, 1964).

As I have noted, Lacan's account of the symbolic register underscores the ability of speech and language to diminish this prospect of openly hostile and violent ego encounters by encouraging conflict to unfold by way of the Other (with a capital o) – that is, via symbolic systems of mediation (see Boothby, 1991: 176–84). Yet Lacan also acknowledges a type of hate that exceeds mediation. That type is one manifestation of what he calls the 'passions of being' that also includes love and ignorance; that is, modes of psychic existence that subsist as deep and intense commitments (see Lacan, 1988: 277). In Lacan's reasoning, hate as a passion of being operates, uniquely, at the border of the real and the imaginary, that is, where one's self-image encounters its roots in the organic forces of the body (see Lacan, 1992: 212). As Recalcati explains (2012b: 57–66), this type of hate is no mere rivalry between egos (or the 'other') but, rather, a rejection of the Other as a mediating point of reference. Hate of that kind, continues Recalcati, is for the Other as such, conceived as a systematic 'way of life' to which the subject is assumed to owe a symbolic debt; and, he claims, it is the distinctive structure of hatreds such as racism (see also Recalcati, 2012c).

What threatens the imaginary ego in this circumstance, Recalcati elaborates, is the full horrifying force of the real – that is, the anxiety-inducing pressure of the subject's own unknowable desire that it has refused in the construction of its identity. Passionate hatred functions as a mechanism to transfigure that threat and project it outward. But in so doing, it aims not – as in a sacrificial logic – to prioritise the Other (understood as a point of intersubjective coordination and exchange), but to reject it altogether. That is because the Other – the ordering of symbolic space as such – is perceived to involve enjoyment *at the subject's expense*; the Other enjoys when the subject cannot and so the subject assumes that it cannot enjoy *because* the Other enjoys. This is the logic of radical hatred peculiar to, for example, the ideologue who directs their anger at civilisation as a whole, conceiving it as the incarnation of an order that systematically exploits and negates the ideals they stand for. In such a scenario, the other (an adversary) is taken to invoke or instantiate the claim of the Other (a structured space of encounter) that threatens to usurp one's own energies. As Recalcati characterises it: 'Hate lashes out against the enjoyment of the Other, against the way the Other enjoys exclusively by stealing it from the subject with impunity' (2012b: 63). To be a subject of hatred, in this sense, is to be opposed not merely to the words and images of a rival but, moreover, to a greedy desire felt to pervade the entire symbolic order.

But how might these reflections illuminate our understanding of the rhetorics of hate? In essence, they point us to a difference between a rhetoric that sharpens imaginary rivalries – for instance, derogatory and insulting remarks between competing politicians and parties that covet each other's perceived advantages and yet often seek the same objects (usually power and influence) – and a rhetoric that rails against 'enemies' purported to usurp the vitality of the group. Each type conjures a distinct relation to the Other and a different way of articulating modes of desire and enjoyment. Both defend against threats to imaginary identity but where the first is, in principle, open to symbolic mediation, the second refuses it; where the first seeks its enjoyment inside the constraints of a shared sacrifice, the second regards enjoyment as something stolen from it and now in the possession of the Other. President Trump's frequent accusations of a 'lying media' propagating 'fake news' approximates precisely this sweeping, hateful rejection of the Other as an intolerable presence with malevolent aims. Yet, in so doing, the subject secretly enjoys its own loss. Passionate haters typically see *themselves* as the true victims (or spokespersons of victims) of a systemic force that goes far beyond mere rivalry – to hate this force is to find deep satisfaction in one's own destitution. That is not to say, of course, that the two types of hate cannot co-exist or even converge with each other. But they offer distinct poles in the spectrum of hate by which to explore rhetorical strategies.

Assessing Labour's Anti-Semitism

If we consider the example of the Labour Party's antisemitism row, we can see both types of hate at work simultaneously. Like any political party, Labour is a broad coalition of groups and interests that identify with particular images of the party's purposes and goals. Each faction promotes its own imaginary identifications as convergent with those of the party as a whole. Intra-partisan rivalry is therefore a common feature of most organisational cultures, especially Labour because it aims to speak for working people as if it were a moral community in need of a unifying voice. This powerful sense of moral purpose is central to the party's ethos and different factions and leaders have always competed to articulate the authentic voice of Labour (Gaffney, 2017). However, recent realignments – associated with the election as leader of veteran left-winger, Jeremy Corbyn MP – have brought many new members to the party and a revival of radical factions and ideals that for some decades had been marginalised. One key motif of these changes has been that Corbyn is felt to open the way to a distinctive, 'new politics' founded on social movements and social struggles against neo-liberalism (see Klug, Rees, and Schneider, 2016). The long-established symbolic structure of the party that has framed it as a broad movement of gradual social reform – already disrupted in light of its loss of governmental power (since 2010) and the collapse of public confidence in its programme and competence – has thus been dealt a further blow by its members' own disenchantment with its general direction in recent years.

One consequence of Labour's realignment around a new leader has been a struggle for positions of power and initiative within the party, often against resistance from opposed politicians and other factions. A new party grouping, named 'Momentum', has attracted a large amount of support among new members by focusing its interest less on the Labour Party's traditionally pragmatic goals and more on the purportedly radical agenda associated with Corbyn. Although he has been on the margins of parliamentary politics for several decades, Corbyn has been widely acclaimed by his supporters as a living symbol of a radical moral stance unwilling to compromise with 'establishment' politics. In the wake of these shifts and conflicts, however, have come verbal aggressions and coarse interchanges between groups and individuals vying with each other in order to diminish or defend a particular image of the party's character and purpose (see P. Martin, 2016; Thompson, 2016). Abusive remarks and hateful attitudes – for instance, accusations from the left of mainstream members being the hated 'Blairites' or, similarly, 'red Tories' – might reasonably be categorised as being of the 'narcissistic rivalry' variety. They represent hostilities among groups with competing (and contrasting) ideas of which offers the most authentic image of the party.

Charges of antisemitism, however, suggest the presence of the second, more intensely hostile type of hate: hate as a 'passion of being'. Complaints of antisemitism arise as a consequence of new members expressing virulently hostile attitudes on foreign policy that are linked to Corbyn's own internationalist agenda, which is heavily critical of the politics of the Middle East and the plight of Palestinians in occupied and heavily securitised areas around Israel. These attitudes demonstrate hostility not simply at individuals but at abstract enemies labelled as 'Zionists' or the so-called 'Israel Lobby', which are accused of having a malign, often undisclosed influence on democratic politics and efforts to achieve justice and equality in the international order, as well as the Middle East. Such accusations and epithets often form part of a wider ideological framework associated with the radical left, which has identified closely with Palestinian causes and deeply mistrusts the policy orientation of western governments towards the region. Connections by western politicians and other advocacy groups to Israel are frequently presented as evidence of complicity with these policies and in contradiction with the left's ambitions for social justice.

What is notable is that this ideological framework does not always resemble the openly antisemitic positions of the far right. So how can it be said to approximate hate towards Jews? It is clearly not the same kind of Jew-hatred we associate with Nazism, which obsessed with the imaginary qualities of the Jews, such as their physiology. For many critics, however, left-wing antisemitism is a relatively new phenomenon with a distinctive rhetoric of its own (see Harrison, 2006; Fine, 2009). The object of hatred is not Jews as such but, more abstractly, Israel and its supporters in the international order, which subjects Palestinians to numerous indignities and injustices. Hateful remarks are therefore addressed by way of the US-led 'imperialist' system – the big Other in this scenario – for which the very existence of Israel and its function as an instrument of a purportedly racially-based colonising power embodies exclusive enjoyment at the expense of Arab communities.

In this anti-imperialist discourse, 'Zionism' is associated no longer as Jewish nationalism but with the greater force of a colonial desire to impose itself on foreign lands, violently robbing and displacing indigenous peoples. This anti-Zionist ideology originated in the emergence of the 'New Left' in the 1950's and 60s and eventually became a touchstone for many of the campaigning organisations of the European left, encouraging arguments that equate Zionism variously with South African apartheid, Nazism, and a host of other injustices of a colonial and authoritarian nature (see Rich, 2016: 31–69). Persistently drawing equivalence between Israel and these regimes (often by openly identifying Israel's policies with Nazism and racism) constructs the undoubted controversies of Israeli foreign policy as evidence of its resemblance with the extraordinary violence of the Holocaust. In making that equivalence, the distinctiveness of the Jews' plight in the 1930s is diminished as a case for understanding the state of Israel. Because these narratives do not dwell on the imagery of Jews as such – that is, because they are frequently addressed to a generic imperialism of which Israel is the privileged instrument – and employ 'Zionist' as a metaphor for an invasive intent, accusations of antisemitism are vigorously disavowed. Criticisms of Israel and its US supporters, it is claimed, should not be mistaken for an opposition to Jews but, rather, a critique of racist injustice.

Such claims and disavowals re-emerged as central threads in the controversy in the Labour Party after 2015: in numerous passing insults and remarks on social media labelling Jews as 'Zio' or associating Israel with American foreign policy (see, for example, Chambre, 2016; Allington, 2018), and explicitly calling for the eradication of Israel from the Middle East; in claims by a prominent Labour activist that Jews 'were the chief financiers of the sugar and slave trade' (quoted in Rich, 2016: 243); in former London Mayor Ken Livingstone's persistent assertion, defended vehemently as 'historical fact', that Hitler and Zionists 'collaborated' with each other in the 1930s (Elgot, 2017); and in other fabricated tales, such as linking Israel to ISIS and Islamist terror crimes (Rich, 2016: 248–9). Although the accumulation of these insults and assertions resulted in a series of scandals (over Corbyn's own controversial public associations and affiliations, for example), suspensions of members from the party and various inquiries, nonetheless some on the left continue to perceive such censure as politically motivated – or given in 'bad faith' – in order specifically and exclusively to undermine Corbyn's leadership (see, for example Davies and Lukes, 2016). Indeed, the very idea of Corbyn as anything other than a virtuous, fair minded anti-racist is treated with ridicule and contempt.

Yet, as critics have argued exhaustively, this disavowal of left antisemitism is hard to accept given the likelihood that Jews (Zionist or not) are those who most identify with Israel. The treatment of Israel and Zionism as substitute signifiers for imperial/racist domination refuses Israel's full legitimacy as a nation state, thereby disparaging the very idea of a historic Jewish homeland and neglecting the historical traumas that brought that state into existence, not only as a nationalist enterprise but as a refuge for Jews who felt abandoned by Europe. The Israeli imaginary – images of Israel as an integral site of ethnic and cultural identification – is therefore dismissed and, for some, its eradication is seen as desirable. Dave Rich (2016: 205) points out that New Left anti-racism has assumed that skin colour was the primary factor in racist discourse; by consequence 'Jews and antisemitism have been gradually squeezed out of popular understandings of what racism is'. Conceived as a uniquely racist and colonial settlement, Israel receives a disproportionate amount of disapprobation for its policies in relation to Palestinians; it is the primary focus for 'boycott and disinvestment' campaigns that are rarely directed at other states, which commit more extensive human rights abuses; and obsessions with similarities and links to Nazism 'remove the moral basis of Israel by suggesting that whatever status and privileges Jews had as victims has been lost' (Rich, 2016: 221). The Israeli state is thereby singled out as a very particular kind of demon: one whose crimes are so malevolent they deserve maximum attention and targeted initiatives (see Hirsh, 2016). Moreover, the tendency on the left to uncritically reproduce well-known conspiracy theories about secret but extensive 'Zionist influence' in western politics and the media, with furtive coalitions organised by the 'Israel lobby', or the financial interests of the Rothschilds and so on are all familiar, traditional antisemitic clichés and tropes that fill out the paranoid fantasy of a malignly constructed world order that must be opposed without further reflection.

The ideological frame within which all these arguments and labels are set borrows its structure from antisemitic discourse, even if Jew-hatred is not the explicit or intended motivation of its advocates. Of course, antisemitism is a familiar formation for rhetorics of hate. As Stephen Frosh argues, this is not merely because it is a convenient form of scapegoating but, rather, the 'Jew is a principle of otherness for the West', a potent, culturally institutionalised figure of excess that functions as a metaphor for all otherness (Frosh, 2005: 215–16). It is therefore conceivable that arguments can be rooted in antisemitic rhetorical formulations without being consciously or aggressively directed at Jews as such (though, in fact, individual Jews and Jewish MPs are regularly singled out as especially accountable for events in Israel). While this structure of hate supplies a powerful motivation for a politics of opposition, its rejection of the symbolic Other (the US-led imperialist order) makes it distinctly resistant to conciliation and fundamentally isolates Jews for whom Israel remains a potent source of cultural identification.

A serious difficulty with this rhetoric is that it cannot even acknowledge itself as hate and therefore engage effectively in dialogue with Jews and supporters of Israel. A whole variety of 'factual' arguments are frequently drawn upon in its defence so as to demonstrate its basis in simple reason rather than unconscious sentiment. To admit that it is desire, not knowledge, that is the source of its rhetorical stance would be to compromise the left's self-image. In part that reflects the rationalistic orientation of the western left, which tends to see its arguments as founded primarily on the evidence of empirical experience and reasoned inference, not radical intolerance. But it is also a consequence of the powerful collective narcissism that the left exhibits when it identifies itself as what David Hirsh (2018: 52) calls the 'community of the good'. Here the imaginary source of one's arguments is conceived as a place of privileged moral authority, unsullied by filthy compromise or complicity with power. However rousing this idealisation of the collective moral self may be, it renders severely limited the possibility for symbolic exchange with those outside it. Indeed, for Hirsh, the contemporary left's recent 'identity politics' – its apparent obsession with who groups *are* and not what they say – increasingly involves what he calls a distinctive 'politics of position': the policing of the boundary of political discourse and the blank refusal of dialogue with those positioned outside. 'That is why, although there are good reasons to worry about antisemitism on the contemporary left, those reasons are not being heard. They are silenced by the shared assumption that anyone wanting to give such reasons is really speaking in bad faith in order to collude with the oppression of the Palestinians' (Hirsh, 2018: 55). Such rhetorical defensiveness on the left tallies with what Recalcati sees as a puritan fantasy – common to this kind of passionate hate – of making a breach with the prevailing order, refusing its dependence upon the Other, and anticipating its wholesale refoundation (Recalcati, 2012b: 60–61).

From Hate to Conciliation

The force of the bitter argument, I have suggested, lies in a capacity to present the excess of desire as a dangerous enjoyment in the other that threatens the subject. In conventional political exchanges this takes the form of vituperative discourse that polices the boundaries of an assumed agreement about the parameters of acceptable speech. But, in hateful speech, it appears as the refusal to occupy common ground and the ascription of radically malign intent to the Other. In the latter case, the very space of argument is brought into dispute and it is hard to find any common measure by which to re-establish exchange. In such circumstances, public argument meets frustration and deadlock.

This is a situation that often prevails among deeply disaffected groups in divided societies who refuse any interaction with those they identify as supreme enemies. But, recently, such antagonisms have entered into the mainstream as political leaders and parties seeking to overturn 'establishment' politics have grown in popularity. President Trump's presidency in the US, for example, is founded on a claim that the Washington elite has long enjoyed itself at the expense of ordinary citizens. As a consequence, Trump's style – honed in his appearances on 'reality' TV – has been to refuse conciliation with the expectations of conventional democratic politics, and thereby to evade the constraints of discursive consistency, respect for opponents, or the general decorum assumed of the leader of a superpower. What is surprising about this type of stance, which builds on an avowed 'hate' of the establishment, is how effective it is as side-stepping external pressure from politicians and the media, which continues to censure him in the name of a common sacrifice that Trump and his supporters refuse. By positioning himself as if outside the established symbolic order, Trump lowers the expectation that his validity be revealed in his conformity with the norms and values to which other presidents have usually shown deference.

But this is not something invented exclusively by Trump. After 9/11, argues Niza Yanay, hatred became 'a rhetorical trope to create legitimacy' (Yanay, 2013: 2) when suspicion of Muslims, the left, and other critics of US foreign policy intensified among state actors, the media and among American population at large (see Butler, 2010; Anker, 2014). In the context of this wider cultural and political affirmation of hateful attitudes and suspicion, Trump's strategy has been to develop a demagogic style focussed on hyperbolic affirmation of a 'victimised' in-group (his supporters) and rejecting a homogeneously conceived out-group (the establishment, the media, people 'not on my side'), utilising confidence in the emotional attachment of his supporters to refuse the legitimacy of conventional decorum and even the validity of criticism (see Roberts-Miller, 2017: 36–66). For some, such divisive rhetoric represents a new form of fascistic politics that recalls the mobilisation of hate against democracy in Germany by Hitler (see Connolly, 2017). Similar strategies utilising hatred to polarise allegiances have also been taken up elsewhere, for example under Viktor Orbán in Hungary, to contest the validity of liberalism, if not democracy itself.

But if such strategies have become more widespread, is the answer to refuse hate and verbal hostility absolutely? Is such a thing possible? Is it even desirable? Although vitriol and hateful speech stir up anger and division, sometimes encouraging threatening and violent behaviour that few would regard as acceptable, closing it down altogether neglects to see what it is often telling us: namely, that the laws, codes and practices that make up the symbolic order are often inadequate, inconsistent, neglectful and even oppressive. Hateful speech and behaviour may produce dead-lock but it remains an effective way to disrupt the presumption of consensus and agreement and to refocus attention on alternative principles around which to rally. If established institutions constantly resist reflection on their own malfunctioning, treating their founding ideals or erstwhile representatives as 'thieves' of enjoyment disengages the symbolic appeal of such institutions. Practices such as slavery, patriarchy, colonialism and so forth were never rationally persuaded to relinquish their grip on society but were held up to passionate criticism, ridicule, and shame by people who encouraged a hatred for them. The virtue of hatred, if we can describe it that way, is that it radically dissolves the aura of intrinsic authority assumed by the Other. It turns the sacred into the profane, diminishing its automatic legitimacy and forcing it onto the defensive. In short, hatred for something in the Other dethrones it (or its representatives) from elevation to a unifying point of reference to be taken for granted. We divest it of the fantasy that it gestures to some missing quality (the *objet a*) and, instead, return it to the status of the Thing, a devouring monster that usurps our strength.

A certain aspect of hatred – its deconstruction of authority – might, then, be fairly regarded as positive in so far as it helps dislodge thoughtless attachment to the symbolic order and its unquestioned trappings. This offers the potential to say more about the institution in question, to expand debate on its functions and to reflect critically on its consequences. Hatred can sometimes open up the parameters of argument to more and unheard voices or ignored experiences. But as a political strategy it also imposes the burden of offering up a new principle and, too often, that is either missing in hateful discourse (so that hate is nihilistic and destructive) or it invests heavily in the intrinsic personal virtues of an individual leader (eg Trump, Corbyn, Orbán) as the locus of a new order (with all the attendant dangers of uncritical devotion). Paradoxically, then, in rejecting what is perceived as a threatening enjoyment in the Other, hate invests its energies in servicing the leader's own unrestrained enjoyment. Regarding the leader, or the 'sovereign' principle he or she represents, as by necessity outside conventional constraints grants the Other substantial, perhaps worrying, leeway to act as it pleases (see Newman, 2019: 98–195).

But is there any way to express hate without abandoning altogether the place of the Other? That is, can we radically contest the structure of the symbolic order without descending into a passionate fury that leaves us uncritically locked into a deaf, self-serving enjoyment?

Interestingly, religious rhetoric supplies an example here: the American tradition of the Jeremiad, for example, where society's spiritual and moral failings in the present are lamented and a prophetic call for renewal is offered up (see Murphy, 2009). This is a style common to Christian fundamentalism in the US but also of civil and political reformers such as Frederick Douglass (see Douglass, 2016) and Martin Luther King (see King, 1999). In the Jeremiad passionate hatred directed at the damaging enjoyment of the prodigal Other is uniquely twinned with hope and the prospect of eventual redemption. In the cases of Douglass or King, the conditions of slavery and racial injustice in America are presented as objects of hate and disgust, markers of a spiritual blind spot in society that demeans all individuals universally and cannot be tolerated. The deficiency of the Other – racist violence in America – is not a mild transgression of norms but a radical contradiction at the very heart of the ideals of freedom and equality. But if the Other's cruelty is rejected, the place of the Other – the notion that there is an inclusive principle that can mediate all differences – is nonetheless sustained. This principle may not yet be instituted but it functions as a moral position from which to judge society. It therefore embraces a principle of sacrifice in order to defend the place of the Other – that is, its structural position in discourse – but it does so by vehemently criticising the current, hateful state of affairs, treating enjoyment not as something stolen but as something yet to be gained.

Of course, the Jeremiad tradition is rooted in a very specific cultural confidence in the original virtues of the founding fathers and their Divine guarantee. But it need not be employed exclusively in support of the Christian principles to which both Douglass and King appeal. A secular approach can be found, for example, in Robert Kennedy's 'The

Mindless Menace of Violence' of 5 April 1968 (see Kennedy, 1968). This was a public appeal in the aftermath of Martin Luther King's assassination, aimed, in the immediacy of the moment, at calming tempers and holding back further bloodshed. Kennedy resists the urge to blame anyone in particular, enlarging the responsibility for social tensions to the whole of society: 'Some look for scapegoats, others look for conspiracies, but this much is clear; violence breeds violence, repression brings retaliation, and only a cleaning of our whole society can remove this sickness from our soul'. Rather than treating loss as the theft of what is rightfully owed to one side rather than another, he refocuses attention on loss itself. Kennedy is not diminishing anyone's responsibility; he seeks to direct attention to the structural violence of social inequality and injustice – 'the terrible truths of our existence' – which creates the context for perpetual hatred and violence. This injustice, he claims, is a spur to invoke a 'common faith' and 'common goal', that is, to refine a social solidarity that rekindles a sense of shared sacrifice and reinvests the Other with an authority founded on conciliation.

Conclusion

Vituperation and hate should not be regarded as fundamentally alien to political discourse. Rather, they are an integral and unavoidable dimension of it. A politics without any insult or hatred is probably not much of a politics at all. We speak in public not merely to exchange information and opinion but to expose each other's imaginary identifications and conceptions of the good life to symbolic mediation. Inevitably that means testing and sometimes exceeding the boundaries of decorum and running the risk of censure in order to refigure the space of discourse. At its most powerful, invective offers a tool to return adversaries to the principles that are held to bind society, clarify the stakes of controversy, and restore public focus. Public speech is thus a combative and bruising experience at the best of times. Yet it holds out the prospect of limiting direct aggression and violence in favour of the sublimated conflict of words. Sacrificing the full and unrestrained enjoyment of our passions and opinions is the price we pay for social peace.

But beyond narcissistic rivalry (which itself can be deeply damaging if left unchecked) hateful speech has the potential to dislodge us entirely from any mediating exchange. I have noted the example of recent debates over antisemitism in the Labour Party to highlight how this kind of hate (hate as a 'passion of being') is manifest as a point of destructive rhetorical deadlock. By definition, rhetorics of hate project their intolerance onto the deeds and ideas of others, disguising the satisfactions such attitudes offer to the haters' own psychic organisation. In such cases, desire is refused rather than recirculated. Antisemitism provides perhaps the cultural template for a type of thinking and speaking about the invasive Other and its exclusive enjoyment at one's expense. But I have also suggested that hate can be a productive source for political dialogue in so far as it enables us to define the stakes and limits of public argument. Taking ownership for what and how we hate – rather than abandoning ourselves to an isolating, narcissistic purity – may involve acknowledging hate as a means to organise desire around a traumatic loss that none of us can escape; and hence as a responsibility to find new forms of dialogue and conciliation. We cannot eliminate hate, but we might find better ways to let our hate speak.

5. An Ethics of Speech?

Can there be an ethical approach to public speech and argument? In recent years, as social and political norms in liberal democracies have come under fire from various quarters, the tone and quality of public discourse has become rancorous, deeply polarised, and on occasion furiously uncivil. Discomforting episodes of public discord come and go in the life of most regimes and, frequently, a common response has been the call to 'raise the tone' of the rhetoric, 'show greater respect' for opponents, emphasise more of 'what we have in common', and so on. Given my emphasis in the last chapter on the uncivil underside of political rhetoric, might we not still hope to readjust the balance and find some way for public speech to promote the common good?

Rhetoric has a mixed reputation as regards ethics. On the one hand, the rhetorical arts are traditionally associated with an orientation towards the good. Rhetoric is understood not as using any old language or communicating in some neutral sense but as participating in a common enterprise and being motivated to achieve morally affirmative outcomes for all. Speech, in this respect, describes a distinctively civic practice that undertakes an ethically positive stance towards disagreement. In part, that is what distinguishes rhetoric from, say, modern linguistics or the various models of 'discourse' theory available today. It is a knowledge designed for the purpose of instruction; hence it is overtly attuned to promoting shared meanings and practices, cultivating respect and a sense of communal integrity, as teachers of the art regularly testify (see, for example, Sinnott-Armstrong, 2018). Yet, on the other hand, it is impossible today to get through a conversation about rhetoric before someone mentions Hitler and presents all the associated evidence that speech, in itself, has no intrinsic moral orientation. If left unchecked, rhetorical skill inexorably leads to grotesque distortions of truth, to tyranny, and injustice. Far from being ethical, speech has more than proved its capacity to help sow social division and nourish discord. Not without good reason, we find it hard today to accept that our smooth-talking politicians or demagogic ranters necessarily have our best interests at heart. And yet, in the absence of any other medium to share and contest social and political values, to formulate policies and articulate our stances towards them, speech remains all we have.

One response to the problem of how to practice speech ethically has been to formulate rules of discourse that set out identifiable norms by which to justify what we say, rather than rely on implicit or assumed standards of good behaviour (see Habermas, 1996a; 1996b: 180–201). In a pluralistic, 'post-traditional' world, where what counts as good or fair speech can easily vary and clash, explicit rules of discourse encourage us to discipline our public conversations in a way that excludes the most malign and provocative rhetoric. A psychoanalytically informed response, on the other hand, is inclined to suspect that any such rules are unlikely to overcome prejudice or mutual suspicion. Indeed, they may even be *more* likely to encourage such feelings under a veneer of 'impartiality'. It is the very notion of the common good, if only in a minimal sense, that is the problem. For rules of good behaviour, like laws generally, alert us to something absent and command us to align ourselves with the Other's prohibitions on the suspicion that we are always guilty of holding illicit desires. For Lacan, as we have noted, desire is strictly bound to the Law. Rules of public speech may, in some pragmatic sense, be worth adhering to. But that does not necessarily make them ethical. Lacan's approach to psychoanalytic ethics, on the other hand, invites us to think not about restraining ourselves for the 'sovereign good' but, rather, of being faithful to the source of our desires. That involves acknowledging that, fundamentally, satisfaction derives not from being in the service of the Other but from encountering limits to our being. Psychic enjoyment, as I have argued, comes from experiencing such limits as a form of loss.

A psychoanalytical ethics, on this view, compels us to take responsibility for our desire rather than compromise it. In what follows, I argue that this ethical demand encourages us to incorporate loss (or the awareness of the intrinsic limits to our being) into practices of public speech. I shall explore this possibility in relation to rhetorics of polemic and testimony by way of instructive examples. But first, let me sketch in more detail the problem of rhetoric and ethics.

No Common Measure

Moral controversies and disagreements are central preoccupations of the rhetorical tradition. Putting one's case, defending its claims, making them meaningful to an audience, adjusting their parameters in light of criticism, and so forth: these are all ways to participate in a public realm marked by differences over what is the right thing to do in matters of common concern. Today, however, we increasingly find that it is *what* we say or how we say it that is itself the cause of dispute. Too often, public disagreements drift away from the matter of what is the best judgement and clash, instead, over what is being said at all and what authority anyone has to say it.

Moral disagreement in contemporary societies, we might say, is increasingly staged not as an interaction between different positions on the same issue but as divisions over what counts as a legitimate opinion in the first place. In public cultures that now exhibit heightened attention to language and the authority it mobilises, disagreements all too readily polarise and bump against refusals to accept that the other can even speak as it does. Moral outrage at the sheer audacity of even saying some things, hostility towards those whose motives we suspect, complaints of callous insensitivity, very often reduced to an accusation of 'racism' or 'fascism', spill from public forums and social media on a daily basis. More and more, experts who claim some authority are abused or dismissed as partial (and therefore unacceptable) sources (see Davies, 2018). In some recent disputes, such as debates over the rights of transgendered people, even suggesting that the term 'woman' describes a biologically sexed category is perceived as 'transphobic' hostility and therefore an utterly unacceptable remark. Obsessions about what people say and what opinions they subscribe to, rather than the quality of their arguments or the contexts of their beliefs, appear to dominate certain layers of public culture with the result that disagreements collapse into angry exchanges of insult or malevolent efforts to disrupt the discourse of those with whom we disagree.

There are, doubtless, many reasons for these types of conflict. Short attention spans in public cultures operating with real-time technologies, the explosion of social media in the last decade or so, and the subsequent narcissistic compulsion to measure all opinions in terms of whether they affirm our personal identities are frequently blamed for diminishing our capacity for 'talk' (see Turkle, 2015). Contributing to this is also the failure of western democracies to sustain the idea of neutral public spheres, as governments and politicians undermine conditions of socio-economic equality and subsume all public policy under calculations of economic competitiveness (Davies, 2018). In such circumstances, the to-and-fro of argumentative positioning increasingly seems like a needless compromise on one's capacity for self-assertion. Despite all the expanding opportunities for individuals to speak and communicate in contemporary democratic cultures, the inability to agree a common measure by which to manage moral disputes means that public debate sometimes resembles more a French Theatre of Cruelty than a forum of engaged interlocutors.

All this is a long way from the expectations of ancient orators and rhetoricians. The classical proponents and teachers of the rhetorical arts took it for granted that speech served to promote the common good. Speech that did not seek this end was, like tyranny itself, a danger to the political community's self-determination. As a civic practice aimed at deliberating and affirming communal goals over personal or partial opinions, speech was expected to be motivated by the moral primacy of the public over the private realm. Teaching rhetoric was therefore, in part, about cultivating citizens worthy of that overriding concern. That didn't mean everyone had to agree the same policies or goals. But even if political and legal disputes could be quite sharp and even dangerously divisive, the orator's dexterity was valued in so far as it was ultimately fastened to the sustenance of the community. Rhetorical skill was thus often conceived as the mark of a virtuous character; eloquence, as well as verbal cunning, displayed one's personal commitment to that end and were therefore signs of a good will (or *ethos*). For the ancients, at least, public speaking made manifest a sense of duty and love for their shared life.

It is hard now not to see this view of rhetoric as somewhat pious and, given the highly factional and often violent politics of the time, rather hypocritical. Plato, among others, judged the self-image of rhetoric to be entirely at odds with its divisive reality. Yet, as a body of knowledge, rhetoric has retained its connection to an assumed civic ethos across the centuries, even when we know it can go very badly askew. It still seems to invoke a mode of speech where the public good – and its associations with virtuous character, active citizenship, or moral duty – are centre stage. Unlike the more contemporary approaches to 'communications', for example, which break down public discourse into separate functioning parts, rhetoric conjures an old-fashioned image of public commitment, integrity and service. Thus one of the underlying threads in rhetorical study is the assumption of an ethical responsibility on citizens to speak, speak well, and to direct one's speech to the elaboration of the good. The polis was an object of strong collective identification – not a neutral arbiter above the political fray but the fundamental premise of all common value.

But it is precisely that shared sense of the priority of the good of the polis that we cannot now assume, even if (because it is largely absent) it may seem quaintly attractive. In the modern age, we do not believe there is a substantial sense of the good to which we all subscribe by virtue of being citizens. Rather, the modern state has been emptied of most of its ethical demands upon citizens. That is not to say there is *no* sense of the good, but what that is is no longer bound up with a substantially shared set of values (see Bauman, 1993). Rather, in highly plural societies, rights – which grant broad personal freedoms – rather than shared morality set the parameters of public authority over the individual. In private life, we can pursue whatever good we prefer so long as it does not infringe on the rights of others. The hollowing out of the ethical content of the state has, of course, created a whole variety of arguments about how moral substance might be reinvested in political authority – from communitarian liberalism and socialism to fascism. But the cost of such efforts is usually a collapse in the very distinction between public and private realms and, therefore it is argued, a threat to 'the primacy of the right over the good' that informs liberal-democracy.

Ethics concern the question 'to what are we responsible?' in any given circumstance. In liberal democracies we tend to think of the base line of our shared responsibility as each other's fundamental rights. Beyond that, the common measure of mutual empathy for our judgements of right and wrong grows fuzzier and is usually based on habit and tradition rather than considered argument. In matters of public discourse, especially, the parameters of acceptable speech and expression – what can be said, what can't, where we should employ euphemism or metaphor, and when we can talk openly and intimately – are rarely little more than flimsy conventions. In the absence of formal enforcement, such conventions are open to flux: something we notice in changing forms of address, for example, or in the naming of distinct social groups. When speech conventions do clash, however, there is no definitive point of reference to determine their 'proper' parameters, that is, to decide what should and should not be said or heard. Disputes within universities and student societies, for example, about who is an acceptable interlocutor, what kinds of argument should be heard, and which should be censured or even refused a hearing (what in the UK is referred to as 'no-platforming') arouse considerable indignation because such decisions can seem so narrow, directed largely at the latest hate figures. Such conflicts produce, in turn, heated arguments about the arbitrary limiting of 'free speech' (heightened by the fact that they occur in universities which are conventionally expected to be robust environments in which disagreement is tolerated).

What is exemplified in disagreements between defenders of 'free speech' (on campus or anywhere else) and those who regard themselves as protecting vulnerable social groups by endorsing censorship (on issues such as hate speech, pornography, and so on) is a clash between different notions of the sovereign good – that is, the overarching moral principle that should inform, if only unofficially, the ethics of speech. For the first, the higher value to which we are ultimately responsible is that all opinions get to be voiced, even if we disagree with them or find them objectionable. For the second, that higher value is the integrity of otherwise marginalised groups, who are frequently the object of denigration and abuse. The difference between the two falls across modern rhetoric's ethical problem: to have a productive disagreement there needs to be some element of agreement – some common ground – already in place about the space of conflict. In ancient society, that space was the polis but in the modern state it is much less certain. Free speech arguments present any such agreement as a minimal one, designed to grant as much liberty as possible to those who want to voice their opinions. Those inclined to censor and constrain public speech, on the other hand, regard the agreement as a 'thicker' one about the priority of group solidarity or human rights.

In the US, this problem is undoubtedly exacerbated by the Constitution's First Amendment which formally prohibits government interfering with the right of free expression. In such conditions, asserting restrictions over what is said in public can be very controversial and defenders of free speech justify their appeal to the First Amendment on the basis that censorship and 'political correctness' are usually obstacles to a healthy 'market place of ideas'. Left unrestricted, free speech enables poor opinions to be exposed and, in the long run, permits good opinions to get a hearing. However, Stanley Fish points out, there is no principle in the Constitution that demands that free expression actually produce an improvement of cultural discourse, nor any logical reason that it will (1999: 93–114). Speech as such 'is never a value in and of itself', he states elsewhere; it is never entirely outside of disputes over the good and hence it is always vulnerable to politics (1994: 104). Speech and expression is necessarily controversial and usually experienced as limiting in some way to someone, so avoiding dispute by appealing to the First Amendment fails to acknowledge that, in fact, 'there's no such things as free speech'. It's only ever a degree of freedom in contexts of choice and interpretation that may favour one side and then, at other times, another. Reliance on a 'higher' principle (whether for or against censorship) usually evades facing up to the existence of political contests over where the boundary lies: that is, 'decisions about what is and what is not protected in the realm of expression will rest not on principle or firm doctrine but on the ability of some persons to interpret – recharacterize or rewrite – principle and doctrine in ways that lead to the protection of speech they want heard and the regulation of speech they want silenced' (110). Fish's argument is that, whatever we regard as the overarching moral priority in the modern state, we cannot ever escape the 'din and confusion of partisan struggle' (115). Such constraints, he claims, are what generates speech and expression in the first place and, by consequence, 'we must take responsibility for our verbal performances – *all* of them' (114).

We are left, it seems, with the ambiguous situation in which the moral regulation of speech is dependent, fundamentally, on a rhetorical politics that itself may be unethical, or at least outside established ethical frames. If we follow Fish's argument, the decision about where to 'draw the line' on what is permissible in public expression – to establish what I have referred to as a 'common measure' – itself comes down to the fortunes of argumentative (and other types of) conflict rather than an appeal to an already agreed higher principle. That is something over which we cannot morally legislate since, by definition, it is our moral parameters that are in question. It is why, over time, the notion of a common measure shifts and tilts in different directions as the contents and parameters of acceptability alter and feed into the practice of public argument. The expansion and contraction of moral frameworks over the centuries has thus been a consequence of ideological struggles and conflicts that challenge and shift the limits of public discourse. The standards and conventions by which societies and communities regulate their speech and other types of expression can never be guaranteed simply by appeal to apodictic principles (based on law or tradition or the mere application of reason) that escape dispute, since these always need to be applied and determined in any specific instance. To be 'responsible' for our discourse, as Fish invites, is not therefore to align with an supreme moral good outside of all politics but to accept that we must constantly work to dispose others towards that good in light of hostile and competing interpretations. In turn, that implies an idea of ethics that is directed not at securing the sovereign good but, rather, at foregrounding the limits of our common being. It is here, I shall argue, that psychoanalytical theory has something to offer.

A Psychoanalytic Ethics

Psychoanalysis has a peculiar relation to matters of ethics. Freud was adamant in his *New Introductory Lectures* of 1933 that the psychoanalytical enterprise, as he saw it, supplied no 'worldview' (or *Weltanschauung*) of its own from which to elaborate a preferred organisation of human affairs, especially one premised on positive, universal features of 'human nature' (SE22: 158–82). For him, psychoanalysis exposed the essential folly of mankind's quest for moral perfection or happiness, especially in its religious and ideological formulations (see SE21: 3–56). The individual was deeply and irresolvably divided, in a condition of conflict that rendered harmonious visions of social order utterly utopian: 'One has, I think, to reckon with the fact that there are present in all men destructive, and therefore anti-social and anti-cultural, trends and that in a great number of people these are strong enough to determine their behaviour in human society' (SE21: 7). If man was not 'master in his own house', then he could hardly be expected to bring order and harmony beyond it. A pessimistic liberal late in life, Freud tended to view the prospects for humanity as contingent upon the balanced reasoning of a fair minded elite able to rise above the passions of ordinary people (see Brunner, 2001). The masses, he even claimed, 'are lazy and unintelligent; they have no love for instinctual renunciation'; they are impervious to rational argument and prone to reactionary, dogmatic and infantile beliefs that damage civilisation (SE21: 7). His view of ethical ideals was therefore fairly suspicious, and psychoanalysis was for him better conceived as an ethically neutral tool of scientific enquiry than one of general moral improvement.

Yet it is also undoubtedly true that Freud believed psychoanalysis could bring advantages to individual human lives, if not perfection or happiness. As a therapeutic practice directed at alleviating personal suffering, psychoanalysis could hardly avoid being ethically oriented in some respect. And there is no doubt that many psychoanalysts following Freud regarded their field as one charged with a radical normative force, often as an enquiry that exposes the deep roots of individual emotional disorders in the psychosocial organisation of society. With attention on the way society represses sexual instincts and thereby generates personality disorders, familial conflict and deep personal unhappiness, psychoanalysts have, inevitably, regarded themselves as inclined to various forms of personal and social liberation. Moreover, liberation is usually conceived to be at odds with the prevailing structures of capitalist society, which are believed to enforce repressive behaviours (see Zaretsky, 2015).

So, on ethics, psychoanalysis is (typically) ambivalent. Moral and political ideals are conceived as symptomatic of repression and a refusal to accept imperfection; and yet, merely revealing this point – especially as part of clinical treatment – itself implies an ethical undertaking that acknowledges our potential to recognise and somehow alter our situation. So, for some, psychoanalysis is driven, if not by an elaborate worldview, then by a sense of the good based on an implicit view of human flourishing (see Lear, 1998); while for others, it absolutely is not (see McGowan, 2013: 5–13). The advantage of Lacan's work is that he finds a way to express an 'ethics of psychoanalysis' without turning it into an overtly moral or political enterprise.

For Lacan, following Freud, psychoanalysis does not offer an ethics of the 'sovereign good'. It has no account of what is universally beneficial or how humans might pursue ideals of perfection. Although analysts are constantly asked to help patients find happiness or to find the sovereign good, the analyst 'knows there isn't any' (Lacan, 1992: 300). In his view, the 'ethics of psychoanalysis has nothing to do with speculation about prescriptions for, or the regulation of, what I have called the "service of goods"' (Lacan, 1992: 313) – that is, the balancing of moral outcomes in order to achieve a harmonious, well-ordered life. Psychoanalysis does not teach us how to be better or more virtuous people. For the principle of the good is a figure that is always structured around a symbolic law and hence requires a master signifier (for example, freedom, solidarity, nationhood). It is precisely society's overt moral standards – the desires of the big Other we internalise as children and thereafter struggle to exemplify in our own behaviour – that divide us from ourselves, however benign and universally accepted they seem. The subject for Lacan, as we have seen, exists as a constant excess to the demands of the Other. Whatever code of good conduct or cherished ideals are on offer will always entail 'the bonds of permanent book keeping', or moral calculations, that only make us feel guilty and force us to service our debt to society by prohibiting our desires (1992: 318). For Lacan, then (and *contra* whole swathes of philosophy and psychoanalytically informed thinkers from Wilhelm Reich to Eric Fromm), psychoanalysis cannot offer an ethics of the universal, sovereign good. Happiness and moral improvement are the language of sovereign power; and such power always entails holding off one's desire for, or adjusting it to fit with, social and political authority (1992: 314–15). Lacan's remark to radical students in 1969 was, notoriously, to refute the idea that a better society could ever be achieved without subscribing to a new symbolic law: 'the revolutionary aspiration has only a single possible outcome – of ending up as the master's discourse [...] What you aspire to as revolutionaries is a master. You will get one' (Lacan, 2007: 207).

But to refuse an ethics of the good is not to reject any and all ethics. For Lacan, if there is an ethical imperative to psychoanalysis it is summed up in the question: 'Have you acted in conformity with the desire that is in you?' (1992: 314). That is, the subject should not give way entirely to the Other and refuse the excessive presence of its own desire. What motivates us most fundamentally, the deeply rooted forces that compel us to identify with societal demands and yet are most particular to our own way of being, should not be ceded. This desire, 'which roots us in a particular destiny [...] keeps returning' (1992: 319). It is the insistent, underlying pulsation in our individual lives that, although it compels us to subscribe to the Other, is nonetheless distinctly 'our business'. But the force of social values and expectations can subdue those often obscure and resistant elements of our singular existence. Psychoanalysis cannot make us happy, but it can help us acknowledge what is most intimate about our personal dispositions and inclinations, as opposed to 'giving ground relative to one's desire' (1992: 321).

It is very hard, of course, to distinguish between the Other's desires and our own. We are, as Lacan argued, constituted in part by the desire of the Other: we want its recognition and so we want what it wants. But, in analysis at least, the opportunity exists to separate out those desires by examining the symptoms of our distress or confusion. In particular, analysis affords a chance to question the fantasies to which we subscribe in order to fill out the gaps in the Other's discourse. These fantasies cover over its inconsistencies and cruelties by reference to ideals, values and images that we do not question. As we have already noted, fantasies adorn the symbolic order with images of fulfilment that are deeply alluring. We submit to certain kinds of moral pressure because symbolic authority is permeated by notions of its intrinsic goodness from which it is hard to withdraw or to counter. Indeed, we are often in thrall to the Other in so far as we remain transfixed by its enigmatic opacity, which encourages us constantly to try to work out what *it* wants from us. In so doing, we end up in sustained anxiety and ignoring that part of our own experience that emerges alongside or even in resistance to the Other. But it is here, in that part of our bodily and intellectual dispositions that cannot fully assimilate to the symbolic Law, that our own desire seeps through.

The 'truth of desire' is not some fully independent personality within us that has been repressed and only needs encouragement to be 'authentically' itself. We can never really be free from the Other (or at least an Other) and the divisions it brings, since we are subjects only by virtue of language and the symbolic order. Lacan's ethical imperative, however, urges us to imagine the subject creating a degree of distance from the Other (and its master signifiers), refusing to be subsumed by its desire and therefore by the fantasies deployed to sustain it. That way we may, as Mari Ruti puts it, 'singularize our desire' by recognising and enhancing the idiosyncratic aspects of our own characters (2012: 50). Ethical responsibility arises from a loyalty to what is distinctively ours rather than to social compliance. That may seem like a rather mild ethical code, especially since it does not aim to overturn society or reinvent the world anew. But in refusing total alignment with any universal moral vision it challenges us to find our own, deeply personal resources to cope with the inevitable anxiety and terrifying uncertainty that psychic life entails, even at the cost of upsetting or disappointing advocates of social harmony (see Ruti, 2014).

Massimo Recalcati goes even further to underscore how this psychoanalytic ethic also challenges us to be responsible *for* our unconscious, that is, for that part of ourselves that we cannot ever master or control and that can be uncivil and indecent. This is a part of our subjectivity that contrasts radically with the idealised images we have of ourselves as virtuous beings; but it remains uniquely ours nonetheless. Rather than neurotically blame the Other (society, our parents, 'the system', and so on) for not making us better people, however, we might acknowledge 'what it is in me that favours, nourishes or arouses the evil that afflicts me' (2007: 31). That is, we might recognise our own complicity with our symptom, the way our frustrations and emotional deadlocks are also a source of unconscious enjoyment. That part of us that destructively sabotages our own plans, ensuring that we cannot adequately align with the Other (and so feel guilt instead) also brings degrees of unconscious satisfaction that, although we may consciously disavow it, permits us to enjoy our loss without responsibility.

By making us assume responsibility for our desire, Lacan's psychoanalytic ethics discourages a retreat into the blameless enjoyment of our symptom. Opening up a distance from the Other, then, permits us to loosen the 'flow' of our desires by not concentrating everything in one place like some total, all-consuming commitment. Likewise, however, it should not be undertaken merely to disavow personal culpability by conceiving oneself as an innocent victim of malign external forces. Indeed, for Recalcati, the wider ethical lesson of Lacan's writing is that we learn to live with the 'paradoxical' nature of desire: that is, its tendency simultaneously to connect us to the Other but also to grant us an independent life that is distinctly ours (Recalcati, 2012a: 186–90). Accepting this paradox – and thereby avoiding the danger of thoughtless enjoyment either in over-identifying with the Other or wholly refusing it – is, undoubtedly, a difficult task and requires that we scrutinise our inclinations and examine how our excesses encourage us to abandon ourselves in order to be fervent defenders of some higher moral principle or victims of cruel and uncontrollable powers. Both options entail the refusal to confront the 'real' of our desire, that is, to acknowledge the mysterious and enigmatic excess that warps our selfhood and drives us along as if we had no choice. Defenders of high moral principle, for example, channel this excess into a kind of 'superego' that insists we enjoy a slavish, self-annihilating attachment to the Other (see Žižek, 1994: 54–85); self-proclaimed victims, on the other hand, partly enjoy their own degradation, identifying with their abandonment to merciless powers. These are, undoubtedly, partial dispositions rather than strict personality types. But they signal a thoroughly unethical refusal to acknowledge the way the subject's desires are bound to an enjoyment that is simultaneously disavowed.

Incorporating Loss: The Rhetoric of Polemic

Lacan's ethics of psychoanalysis is not, I have made clear, an ethics of the sovereign good – that is, an ethics that builds upon a defined idea of what is universally good and that prohibits our desires in order to achieve it. That is not to say that such an ethics is *never* worth having. But it is not, for Lacan, one that can be derived from psychoanalytical thinking, which attends to the very singular experiences and intimate motivations of individual subjects undergoing clinical treatment. But what can this ethics offer our understanding of situations beyond the clinic? In the world of public culture and political discourse, how might we act ethically in this sense? I want to suggest that Lacan's ethic invites us to acknowledge loss as the *source* of our satisfaction, rather than an obstacle to be overcome. That way, distance is opened between the source of desire and the Other in whose direction it is inevitably channelled. Incorporating loss – that is, accepting loss as an ontological condition in our rhetorical dispositions, rather than a contingent imposition – can thereby promote an ethical approach to public discourse that might be incorporated in various ways.

For Todd McGowan (2013), as we have seen, the wider lesson to be taken from Lacan's insights (and from psychoanalysis in general) is that no sovereign good can ever harmonise the subject to society. No set of moral prescriptions, political programmes or ideologies will actually reconcile the subject to the demands that society makes on it because, by definition, those demands divide it against itself, constituting the subject as an impossible entity. A psychoanalytical political theory – especially one based on the centrality of the death drive – therefore evades the moralising fantasies that typically motivate political programmes and the speech of politicians and activists. Instead, psychoanalysis underscores 'the indissoluble link between our enjoyment and loss' (2013: 22). Rather than prescribe visions of moral integration or offer designs for a well-ordered society, it accepts that loss, division and dissatisfaction are the precondition for being a subject. It is the ontological incompleteness evoked in loss that produces an orientation to justice, for example. The very absence of satisfaction disposes us towards fantasies of the good and thereby gives us an indirect enjoyment by way of a perceived loss.

So does a psychoanalytic political theory simply tell us to throw up our hands and declare that nothing can be done, that we *need* to feel injustice to be political subjects and therefore we should leave things as they are? Not at all. But it does encourage us to think of the limits of our being as internally rather than externally generated (McGowan, 2013: 284–5). That is, we are ineluctably drawn to what we cannot attain, and it is this unachieved attainment that produces the intense attachment to the good as a goal always yet-to-be-achieved. While we may then imagine that the good is inaccessible only because some empirical obstacle blocks it, in fact its allure arises from the unconscious enjoyment activated by its very absence. Beneath our avowed ideals and detailed visions of the 'better society' our vital energies gather around a gap that functions as the absent cause of our desires. The important manoeuvre, however, is to thematise loss as the inescapable horizon of desire, that is, to understand how empirical impediments, life's vicissitudes and disruptive situations release subjects from the unthought attachments or assumptions that they once took for granted – such as the presence of global capitalism, or the permanence of personal freedom – rendering themselves suddenly responsible for how they manage their emotional investments. Rather than directing their energies towards vanquishing an opponent, subjects can instead experience such limits as provocations to address the structure of their own enjoyment.

A psychoanalytic ethics or politics, then, is a uniquely anti-utopian politics (see Stavrakakis, 1999: 110–12; McGowan, 2013: 283). That is not because it refuses us permission ever to imagine new and different kinds of society. Rather, it is because, at its root, psychoanalysis tells us that the satisfaction we seek arises not from the objective validity or the eventual realisation of the social transformations we demand but, instead, from our capacity to encounter limits to our being. Enjoyment derives from confronting these limits, so to imagine overcoming them in a new society will always fail to achieve the anticipated satisfaction, happiness or fulfilment. We may find relief, for sure, but we will also find new limits with which to identify. Instead, McGowan continues, if we acknowledge loss as internal to the organisation of subjectivity, a condition that cannot be removed but only managed differently, then our attitude towards our ideals and those of others might be radically altered in a way that does not lead us so readily to punishing ourselves and others. That is to say, the ethical imperative in Lacan's theory invites us to rethink all our political projects and the way our investment in them derives neither from the intrinsic value of the goal nor the authority of the Other (science, God, national or cultural tradition) that is served by our commitment. Rather, it comes from the way we organise our drives by registering the limits to our selfhood (our identities, ambitions, political aspirations). Instead of serving the Other, or blaming it for all our woes, we can instead accept loss not as an external impediment but as part of our own psychic constitution.

But what does this formulation imply for how we conceive the ethics of public speech? There are two related but distinct levels to how we might explore the implications: first, that of the space of rhetorical encounter; and, second, that of specific rhetorical strategies we may take up within that space.

To incorporate loss into the social space of rhetorical encounters is to refuse to give primacy to any specific body, individual or collective, as the guide to how speech should unfold. That is to say, it is to insist that nothing but a contingently assembled community is the source of authoritative judgements. That, as we have seen, is how Claude Lefort conceived the emergence of modern politics – as the disincorporation of power from divinely appointed monarchs and its substitution by the idea of power as an 'empty place'. It means that the *place* of the Other still exists – symbolic authority remains, in principle – but it has no (or only minimal) pre-given qualities except those ascribed contingently by whoever occupies that place. Power is thus founded on an absence rather than a presence, ensuring that no occupant can ever lay permanent claim to it. Removing the substantial dimensions of power enables a more democratic and pluralistic type of discourse because it substantially expands the number and variety of participants who may compete to occupy or influence the place of power.

The notion that political power is fundamentally an empty place that is only ever contingently filled has been important to radical democratic theorists, many of whom draw upon both Lefort and Lacan's ideas. The Lacanian theorist, Yannis Stavrakakis, for example, argues for a 'post-fantasmatic' politics as the basis to radical democratic demands for a more inclusive and diverse politics (1999: 120). By rejecting visions of democratic community founded on the presence of a substantial essence that homogenises citizens in advance of democratic encounters – an essence given in fantasies of national identity, for example – Stavrakakis rejects what he calls the 'ethics of harmony' (1999: 121) such visions invoke. Instead, a more diverse and conflictual space of encounter permits a multiplicity of demands and values to interact because no imaginary body determines in advance who is a participant or precisely what may be said. This version of radical democracy supports and is influenced by the work of Ernesto Laclau and Chantal Mouffe (1985). Mouffe's political theory, in particular, rejects the deliberative democrats' insistence that reason and rationality are prior requirements for genuine democratic encounters (see Mouffe, 2000). For her, such a demand aims to found democratic ethics on the presence of qualities that, in her view, substantialise the body of citizens by selectively endorsing certain qualities (often favouring men or certain types of argumentation, for example) that, moreover, incline a democratic community towards an assumed consensus and away from conflict.

For Laclau and Mouffe, a democratic community is premised on the presence of antagonism, or the radical exclusion of certain existential threats (1985: 152–9). It is this antagonism – a sense of the global limits to our collective being – that temporarily stabilises a democratic order, conferring on the multiplicity of contrasting group differences an imaginary unity (or 'equivalence') figured around a frontier defined by its exclusion of a generic 'enemy'. That enemy may consist, for example, of bankers, racists, or religious fundamentalists. Together these enemies supply antagonists that bring together diverse groups and organisations as temporary 'friends' in democratic struggle (Mouffe, 2000: 13). Of course, all communities are founded on some types of exclusion. But by contrast with essentialist approaches to identity, a radical democratic politics acknowledges that the community is constituted through its dissociations rather than treats antagonists as empirical obstacles to its authentic realisation. A radical democracy is therefore premised not on prior consensus but on a shifting alliance of diverse groups unified by what is construed as a common threat. The radical democratic community builds upon this 'absent presence', as Laclau (1996: 42) puts it, that is, a unifying political fiction or 'hegemony' generated by investing excess energies into a common figure of loss.

How does this idea of incorporating loss into a project of radical democracy influence the kind of rhetorical strategies we may endorse? Mouffe's own recommendation is for a conflictual politics that centres practices of disagreement and difference. This is a type of 'agonistic' politics that underscores disputation as the marker of democratic interaction. If there is no sovereign good then politics is charged with the task of arguing out differences, actively articulating what is held in common: by presenting, critiquing, and defending contentious claims. In short, we might characterise radical democratic rhetoric by reference to polemical strategies that figure lines of demarcation between radically competing identities and ideals. That is not, Mouffe argues, to refuse the possibility of consensus at all: a minimal amount of agreement is required for politics to occur on a common terrain. But she underscores that this can only be a 'conflictual consensus', or what she calls (in response to Stavrakakis) 'an ethics of dis-harmony', where alternative visions of the good, rather than an urge to come to final agreement, are given primacy (see Mouffe, 2000: 137). That way, the limits of common being are constantly underscored. In Mouffe's view, emphasising conflict as the horizon against which differentiated positions form temporary hegemonic formations is preferable to a fixed image of what unifies them (such as assumed notions of good citizens, civility, equality, freedom). Always conscious of the possibility that polemical divisions might transform into outright hostility and even violence, Mouffe suggests that democratic community be formed around an open engagement with perceived 'adversaries' – opponents with contrasting ideals but not outright enemies who threaten each other's existence. That way, a polemical, conflictual rhetoric invites opposing visions of social order to clash openly, for passionate disagreement to soak up the excesses of identity without subscribing to exclusionary fantasies of order, implicit agreement or moral wholeness, and for alternative visions of society to be channelled into contingent but workable alliances and agreements rather than fashioning democracy in such a way as to permanently exclude opponents.

Mouffe's defence of agonistic democracy incorporates loss by rejecting rigid parameters of inclusion and, one may infer, by endorsing polemical forms of argument attentive to the limits to consensus. But there is a presumption in both Laclau and Mouffe's writings that radical groups and social movements will acknowledge that their identities are indeed constituted through antagonism. That is, they will recognise their motivations as contingent upon the enjoyment they generate around loss rather than taken to be indications of a pre-political or essential identity merely blocked by a rival. But we might reasonably ask if such groups and movements really do this. While some may, it is not obvious that all do or can do so without rethinking their own politics. Many forms of radical politics include people who believe a 'true' identity will actually be realised once the interference from homophobes/capitalists/imperial oppressors, and so on, are defeated. Indeed, much of the radical left remains committed to the view that overthrowing capitalism – whether in the name of the working class or under the more inclusive category of 'the people' – will bring genuine and universal satisfaction. As a consequence, the commitment to a non-essentialist ethics and diverse alliances may be more pragmatically instrumental than categorical. Left-wing politics is notorious for its tendency to factional conflicts and divisive disagreements (and then splits) precisely because the commitment to universal values, founded on 'objective truths', and non-negotiable group demands exceeds any common principle of loss and mutuality.

Here we can see the limitations of Mouffe's friend/enemy model of politics, which is premised on the idea that the social bond is constituted through exclusion. As McGowan argues: 'The enemy transforms an ontological phenomenon – loss within the social order – into an empirical one – instances of loss' and this 'facilitates the belief that [...] an authentic social bond is something we might have' (McGowan, 2013: 157). In McGowan's view, this position exemplifies what Lacan describes as a 'masculine' logic of sexual identity (see Lacan, 1998: 71–4). Male identity is constructed, accordingly, around the idea of accessing enjoyment by reference to an 'exceptional' figure – the non-castrated male who accesses the phallus and freely enjoys, unlike everyone else. Male identities aim to occupy the place of the exception, to monopolise the sources of enjoyment by eliminating any other exceptional figure and taking up its status (McGowan, 2013: 155). In that respect, a friend/enemy politics involves identifying an antagonist whose illicit enjoyment prevents society from truly enjoying itself. In privileging exclusion, McGowan believes Mouffe's model of radical democracy invokes the possibility of actually enjoying, or fully realising, a harmonised identity. The recognition of loss is thus undercut by the assumption that what is lost can, eventually, be redeemed. And it is such a promise that accounts for the way left-wing groups and organisations (but not only them) constantly fracture as they insist on the objective validity of their own version of the enemy. Working with the illusion that a truly exceptional form of leadership might overcome the generic cause of all exploitation and division, radical left politics often produces lively, diverse and polemical discourses but, nonetheless, frequently culminates in deadlock and accusations of 'betrayal'.

Incorporating Loss: The Rhetoric of Testimony

An alternative mode of incorporating loss, however, is posed by Lacan's model of female sexual identity. Female sexuality, argues Lacan, instantiates a principle of 'not-having' rather than having the object of enjoyment (see McGowan, 2013: 157–9). Female identity is structured, not by the ideal of non-castration or striving to be the exception, but by being 'not-whole', thus recognising that having is really having nothing (Lacan, 1998: 72–3). The identity of Woman is, Lacan asserts, not a universal based on distinct qualities in the way that the Universal Man is often taken to be: 'There's no such thing as Woman, Woman with a capital *W* indicating the universal' (1998: 72). As such, female enjoyment is defined by a very singular sense that no attainable object can ever fully satisfy, and so none is worth pursuing above all else. The model of enjoyment offered by female subjectivity, as McGowan notes, is 'the enjoyment of a shared not having' (2013: 158). It is less a coherent design for a social order and more an acknowledgement that beneath all constituted orders (that is, those based on the exception) is a layer of sociality where loss is impossible to overcome (2013: 159). That is to say, the trauma of being an incomplete subject can never be resolved and thus no friend is ever truly a friend and no enemy ever an enemy once and for all.

In the logic of female sexuality (which, to be sure, is not the same as saying 'all women'. Just as male sexual identity is not exclusive only or to all biological men), loss is not captured by a politics aiming to hegemonize a multiplicity of groups and so produce a movement unified in its hostility to the exception. Rather, loss is encapsulated in an open-ended mutuality occasioned simply by the release from such a presumed unity. We might see this as a loosely organised 'community' based simply on sacrifice. It might even be viewed as a kind of community of suffering, where the social bond, such as it is, is bound closely to a moment of loss. The rhetorical space based on this bond of suffering is more that of the support group, where speech is relinquished of a responsibility to align strictly to the Other, than a political organisation where a common endeavour is foregrounded. In support groups, speakers divulge personal reflections, make confessions, and recount experiences around traumas, which remain singular and intimate. Everyone is an exception in this scenario since everyone has their own intimate and idiosyncratic ways of feeling and talking about feelings –

and the opportunity to talk is never aimed at a substantive collective goal. Instead, satisfaction is experienced primarily in acknowledging loss itself.

By definition, the model of enjoyment based on female sexuality barely matches any overtly political practice since it affirms enjoyment for its own sake rather than as a prelude to actually attaining an object. This disposition is articulated in recounting the experience of trauma, where the impact of a devastating, painful experience is given space and time to unfold in narrative form. It is the rhetoric of testimony, where witnesses to catastrophic events speak of the violent and horrific experiences that have wounded them. As Cathy Caruth suggests, in testimonies of trauma the story of one's life is bound inextricably to 'the story of death' (of one's relatives, for example, or of threats to oneself) (Caruth, 2016: 8). The wounds of trauma – of systematic violence and murder, but also of natural disaster – typically haunt 'survivors' throughout their lives, preventing them from fully engaging in the post-trauma world. To hear testimony is thus to let speak a voice (sometimes of guilt, anger, or sheer horror) that utterly refuses to be compromised by the Other. In this, loss binds itself tightly to the subject as an inescapable dimension of one's being. Bernard-Donals and Glejzer point out in relation to victims of the Holocaust that testimony frequently arises when survivors have been rendered speechless by horrific and terrifying events which, nonetheless, leave them with a powerful, irresistible compulsion to speak (see Bernard-Donals and Glejzer, 2001: xi–xii).

To recount suffering – one's own or that of others – is often to speak of experiences that cannot be assimilated to one's normal self or common ways of communicating; these are experiences of situations that are, strictly speaking, unknowable since, as 'witnessed' events, they are nonetheless so overwhelming and out of proportion to regular life as to defy ordinary measurement. Here, the trauma resembles the experience of what Lacan called 'the Thing', discussed in Chapter 3. The witness *must* give testimony precisely because what has been seen *cannot* be known or represented in ordinary speech. Witnesses thus often feel powerfully drawn to approximate within speech something that, in itself, cannot adequately be grasped. Consequently, continue Bernard-Donals and Glejzer, we should not treat such testimony as the presentation of the factual 'truth' of an event, in an epistemological sense, for the subject is talking about something that is usually at the limit of all sense, an 'excess ... that can only be indicated' (2001: x). Testimonial speech will often fail, for example, or fall into euphemistic evasion, stuttering gaps, even silence. But it is in its failure as factual discourse that a different truth emerges. This truth is the absence or loss of any stable reference to one's being. The rhetorical *ethos* of the giver of testimony is not that of someone whose moral authority derives from their role as an unassailable 'expert witness'. It may instead derive from a capacity merely to indicate what can never be known (see Bernard-Donals, 2000).

The rhetoric of testimony can be vexed and ambiguous because it demands an ethical responsibility to tolerate loss and failure in oneself and others – to accept loss as the pre-condition of speech. Projects of national reconciliation following long periods of violence and injustice, for example, frequently look to the giving of testimony as a way to come to terms with traumatic events and to find satisfaction by acknowledging how our desires may have overwhelmed us. For example, the project of 'truth and reconciliation' in post-Apartheid South Africa in the 1990s exemplified an important effort to establish a non-partisan space of disclosure for those who had committed crimes or suffered as victims of those crimes (see Burton, 2016). Here the primary goal was not simply to judge criminality (as in a regular court of law) but, moreover, to set about healing the personal and communal damage brought by Apartheid for many decades in order to facilitate social reconciliation. Indeed, 'reconciliation' through dialogue was a central rhetorical principle in the whole process, which aimed at generating a wider climate of forgiveness and mutual understanding instead of vengeance or silence (see Doxtader, 2001).

The goal of the Truth and Reconciliation Commission (TRC) was in fact simultaneously legal, political and ethical. By offering legal amnesty, the TRC afforded opportunities for individuals to forego normal forms of criminal justice by confessing to politically motivated acts of illegality and violence for which they would, if sufficiently evidenced, go unpunished. Public hearings, but also written statements, brought to light much of the dreadful, dehumanising force through which the Apartheid regime was sustained. But, in so doing, it sought to initiate a process of reconciliation – though not wholesale societal harmony – by permitting individuals from all sides (security forces, anti-Apartheid militia, political parties and so on) to disclose the excesses of their own actions, to show contrition and offer apology, to take responsibility and even participate in making reparations. In that way, as Doxtader argues, the TRC supported the political transition to multi-racial democracy in South Africa by negotiating a relation between the past and the future. By exploring past experiences through testimony, it was possible to transcend some of the otherwise unacknowledged pain and suffering that many people had endured (2001: 247). The TRC, he goes on to say, thus enabled the movement from the past to the future by making reconciliation a 'dialogical event' and by functioning as 'both a sponsor and performer of public argumentation' (2001: 252).

Of course, the TRC's efforts could only facilitate a process, not bring about lasting reconciliation. It was certainly an uneven experience and, inevitably, much 'truth' remained frustratingly undisclosed (see Leebaw, 2011). Critical doubts therefore linger about the effectiveness of the Commission and its validity for other post-conflict contexts (see Burton, 2016: 116–43). In this instance, public testimony was incorporated into a wider process that aimed quite explicitly at the 'public good' of national reconciliation, and not at disclosure simply for its own sake (Doxtader, 2001: 252). As such, it was a way of incorporating loss that, nonetheless, connected closely to the instrumental purpose of contributing to a peaceful political transition to a new regime. The policy of amnesty was therefore deeply controversial (especially for those who wanted to see criminal justice proceedings for perpetrators of violence) and not uniformly effective, since not all trusted the objective of 'transition'. The rhetoric of testimony nevertheless offers one way that we might understand how to incorporate loss into public discourse according to a female logic: namely, by rhetorically performing the bond generated by trauma.

Negotiating Rhetoric's Ethics and Politics

The contrasting orientations of male and female logics discussed above seem to pit against each other two different kinds of ethical disposition. Each incorporates a general disposition of loss – and, importantly, the satisfaction we take from experiencing loss – thereby opening up a distance between the subject and the Other. This distance offers space for subjects to acknowledge the distinctness of their desire and the psychic enjoyment to which it is connected, without fully compromising with the Other. In rhetorical terms, I have suggested these are encapsulated in polemical and testimonial types of speech, each of which addresses itself avowedly to an awareness of the limits of being: types of rhetoric that acknowledge how desire is motivated by psychic loss itself and by reducing our expectation that loss might be redeemed. These are not the only types of rhetoric that exemplify male and female logics, but they do help clarify what is at stake. Rather than underline the necessity of an official 'norm' to be enforced, the ethic involved here has an informal function. The satisfaction on offer is not one that can be officially mandated or even directly acknowledged without losing its force. To do so would be to objectify loss, to transform it from a disposition into a symbolically quantifiable or exchangeable good. That would lead to disputes over who has suffered the greatest loss or whose sacrifices are most worthy of recognition, which are likely to be ethical dead-ends. Loss – and the psychic enjoyment associated with it – is often more effective when it remains on the margins of discourse rather than at its centre.

What is also clear from the discussion above, however, is that it remains hard to imagine loss without the prospect of gain – that is, a practice of ethics without *some* kind of politics. Even if loss is a source of psychic satisfaction, separating it from the Other as such remains difficult. As we saw, polemic almost always directs arguments to some imaginary resolution, that is, some potential hegemonic principle where all injuries may be healed. Even rhetorics of testimony (where the sheer weight of suffering is foregrounded) are usually supported by encompassing visions of justice, reconciliation or forgiveness that sketch visions of future social order and hence some collective identity perceived to benefit. It is possible, of course, to hold off what that shared identity is in any detail and so maintain a degree of space for multiple imagined futures. Yet it seems impossible to conceive of wholly separating the experience of a sacrificial loss from images of the social bond that it may, if only faintly, adumbrate.

In McGowan's Lacanian terminology, this balance of ethics and politics is one of enjoyment and pleasure. We enjoy loss because its invocation draws us to psychic limits and thereby produces the satisfaction of overcoming ourselves. But we experience a more concrete pleasure when we give definition to the collective social identity that is produced in the wake of shared trauma, compromising the singular intensity of grief or pain so as to align with others. While analytically separate, in reality enjoyment and pleasure are closely intertwined in public cultures, as memorials to national mourning so often indicate: specific experiences of tragic suffering are recalled and, simultaneously, perceived as indicative of a distinct 'national substance' that unifies some (and not others). Ordinary political rhetoric and public speech tend to manoeuvre between the two poles signified by testimony and polemic, pragmatically negotiating a relation between recollections of the traumas that bring subjects into public presence and the political programmes that articulate that suffering as a shared project (see Alexander, 2012). Political speech, I noted in an earlier chapter, frequently draws on tragic moments of suffering and hears the testimony of witnesses and survivors; but it also tries to direct the force of those experiences into political narratives that answer loss with images of the positive social bond produced through them.

The more ethically-oriented such rhetoric is, we might say, the more it tends to hold open the painful experience of loss without trying to mold it into an integral vision of society around a principle that purports to unite the people as one. At its least ethical (or most political), however, partisan divisions form around experiences of loss, aiming to appropriate them according to exclusionary principles of social order. For example, recent nationalist rhetoric gives priority to certain experiences of injury and trauma, in contrast with the frequently inclusive and 'cosmopolitan' arguments that prioritise 'human rights' in the name of a rather indistinct notion of 'compassion' for all (such as in the South African TRC example). In such instances, very particular memories and experiences of suffering become highly motivational resources for 'antagonistic' recollection (see Cento Bull and Hansen, 2016: 393–4). Moreover, the consequence of such selective and instrumental acknowledgement is to fold the experience of sacrifice into exceptionalist fantasies of national redemption. These involve simplistic divisions of 'victims' versus 'perpetrators', 'good' versus 'evil', and imply that, once the preferred group has properly achieved power, it can finally redeem loss, which was caused only by the empirical presence of the antagonist.

It is unrealistic to think that any incorporation of loss into a rhetorical stance will entirely evade controversy or avoid inclining towards some social arrangements over others. Whether it is the memory of the Shoa or more recent examples of genocide, terrorism, catastrophe or civil unrest: disagreement and debate is always likely to occur about what has been lost, who has suffered, and what conditions and agents brought about these circumstances. Even if it is not reducible to it, the ethical moment is rarely wholly separable from the political moment, or partisan argument and advocacy. Rather than think in terms of wholly different types of rhetoric (polemic versus testimony) we might do better to think of them as intertwined dimensions which make available the space to think of loss *and* invite opportunities to channel it towards a moral or political horizon that prioritises some ways of recognising it over others. That is to say, the gap between incorporating loss and invoking a collective body from the experience of loss is the site at which decisive rhetorical action occurs. It is here that an ethico-political choice – and hence responsibility – is to be made over how to articulate the public significance of devastating experiences: by endorsing their singularity (as we do when we step back to allow people to grieve over personal losses) or by treating them as exemplary of society's relation to the Other.

Conclusion

The answer to the question about how to speak ethically, posed at the start of this chapter, is therefore quite different from that made by other approaches to discourse ethics. These tend to recommend idealised images of dialogue or 'deliberation' based on positive moral visions with which speakers are then encouraged to align. Instead, an ethical approach to speech built on an account of Lacan's psychoanalytical theory is one that acknowledges that the urge to speak (or to have others speak for us) emerges from a subjective encounter with the limits of our being, often experienced as loss. Rather than make ethics a matter of aligning speech to shared moral principles, it suggests that we make it a matter of orienting our discourse to the forces within us that compel us to speak. This approach underlines a distinct change of direction in ethics, from attention to something known about the universal (the Other) towards a concern for something unknown in the subject.

That is not to say that moral principles don't ever serve a practical, 'external' function. But as a starting point for speech, by necessity they divide subjects from themselves and encourage them to police divergences from principle. By contrast, a psychoanalytic ethics opens up the distance between the Other and subjective desire, giving ground to the subject to reflect upon its own motivations without insisting on an overarching objective. In many ways, that involves simply offering space to be heard so that the traumas, injustices and exclusions that make us want to speak are not quickly folded into rigid ideological programmes: a position exemplified, in different ways, in rhetorics of polemic and testimony. What is 'ethical' here is not a matter of insisting on standards of 'good behaviour' or 'civility' – which are ways of disciplining desire – but an invitation for subjects to resist being consumed by utopian attachments or destructive anger at opponents. It will not filter out all passions and hostilities, but it can serve to lessen the pressure to identify or to concentrate all one's energies in one object. Which is to say, it holds out the prospect that we might take responsibility for our own motivations rather than project them on to others. That way, we are encouraged to regard the limits to our being – which is what compels us to find a voice for our desire – as the 'internal' condition to the rhetorical stances we adopt and something for which we are, as singular subjects, always responsible.

Conclusion

Social and political anxieties regularly play out as preoccupations about public speech. We squabble over what can and cannot be said, who ought to be heard, and who should not. Whether in disputes over 'bad' language, the 'incivility' of our discourse, the 'erasure' of marginalised identities, or just the malign intentions and mistaken priorities of our institutions, public argument is so often turned inwards to lament its own, unsatisfactory shape. In the midst of our outrage, all too frequently we end up arguing about the way we are arguing and not so much about specific problems or issues. Such controversies can be distracting and, ultimately, fruitless. But they also suggest that what is going on in speech is never merely the practical resolution of discrete problems but, moreover, the way we inhabit a shared world and wrestle with our desires within it. A psychoanalytical approach to rhetoric, I have argued in this book, directs itself to the processes by which public speech and argument struggle to dispose subjects coherently towards their worlds. It looks to public controversies and disputes as efforts to contain and channel the excesses of subjectivity by activating desire and managing psychic enjoyment. In this respect, rhetorical strategies manifest what I have described as a 'psychopolitics of speech'.

In these concluding remarks, I want briefly to summarise the argument as it has developed chapter by chapter and to invite further reflection on how rhetoric and, in particular, the experience of loss are bound together.

The Flesh of Argument

To think of arguments as ways to figure desire is not to deny that disputes and disagreements have an ideal or conceptual character. But it is to suggest that language and conceptuality never exist entirely independently from the individual and collective bodies that produce them or to which they are addressed. In Chapter 1, I claimed that speech and argument might usefully be approached by way of Merleau-Ponty's notion of the flesh. The flesh is not the material body as such but, rather, the elemental continuity of perceiving subjects with the material and social world – this continuity involves multiple layers of texture and sensation in relation to which conscious awareness subsists only as a momentary and selective response. Speech, rhetoric and argument, from this perspective, are modes of attending to, but also resisting and controlling sensual possibilities; folding subjectivity into abundant wells of feeling, smoothing over or even recoiling from them. By drawing attention to particular objects within our spatial and temporal horizons, magnifying some parts and diminishing others, connecting and separating ideas, principles and events, rhetorical discourse puts us in and out of touch with the unconscious fleshy underside of human experience that we otherwise screen out of view. To conceive of speech this way is, at very least, to acknowledge a carnal politics at work in how we speak and argue, and not to displace language into the frictionless world of abstract ideas or 'representations'.

In Chapter 2, I expanded on the intertwining of mind and body encapsulated in the idea of the flesh by turning to the insights of psychoanalysis. Freud, I suggested, offers an implicit theory of persuasion in his account of how the psyche copes with the powerful forces of its own bodily drives. In psychoanalytical thinking, the force of the flesh is channelled through psychical mechanisms that repress, deny, or displace it into a largely unconscious realm. Our psychic lives are organised through the unsteady management of desires that exceed conscious control and run up against our conscious egos. Public argument is therefore one medium for the restraint and release of desires into the 'plausible stories' that moderate our relation to the flesh. Lacan's work, I continued, clarified this view by looking to the way language articulates and sustains desire. Yet, caught in the grip of the signifier, the subject is by consequence never fully in charge of its own voice. Moreover, it is persistently fending off the challenge of the death drive – or what Lacan calls the 'real' – to the precarious object known as the ego.

The way that speech and argument fold the flesh into specific modes of seeing (and hence inhabiting) the world was the focus of Chapter 3. The dynamic of imaginary, symbolic and real registers in Lacan's work, I claimed, could be conceived as a theory of argumentative disposition. By transforming subjective excess into a rhetorical stance, Lacan's theory of discourse illuminates the operations of fantasy (via the *objet petit a*), understood as a mode of figuring absence as an alluring lost object. In so far as they assemble, break apart and reassemble discourses, rhetorical practices instantiate a process of figuring the lost object that aids the inscription of subjects into the symbolic order. In this, rhetoric is tasked with encountering the real of desire while remaining at a safe distance from it. Such an approach recasts the analysis of the 'rhetorical situation' as the retroactive cause of the subject's desire and draws attention to the way political speech seeks out the stain on its perceptual horizons.

Addressing Loss

In the first three chapters I moved from the idea of speech being bound up with the flesh to the notion of subjectivity as an experience of excess; and then to the claim that rhetorical discourse is a medium to manage desire by figuring loss. In the next two chapters, I explored how a number of different types of rhetoric figure this loss. In Chapter 4, attention was given to the force of vituperation and insult in political cultures. To a great extent, the uncivil character of political language is a function of an ongoing urge to enforce a certain recognition of sacrifice, or shared loss, as the precondition for civil relations. We get to speak and listen to each other because we forego enjoying a satisfaction without limits and adhere, instead, to the strictures of the Other. The cruelty and sharpness of much language is a response to the suspicion that others are enjoying illicitly by not restraining themselves. Hateful language and uncivil conduct is thus an integral feature of political life. But when the discomforts of sacrifice for the Other is replaced by a hatred of the Other as such, enjoyment is taken in refusing sacrifice.

Finally, in Chapter 5 I looked at how loss could be addressed in an ethical (rather than moralising) approach to speech. Drawing on Lacan's account of psychoanalytic ethics I argued that rather than refusing loss, or blaming it on the Other, it might instead be incorporated into an ethical rhetorical disposition. That meant thinking of loss as something that constitutes the subject *as desiring* and not as a subject that can ever attain its object. To instil an ethical attitude in this respect means generating a productive distance between the subject and the Other. I set out two ways that we might think of this: in the form of polemical rhetoric, where loss, conceived as antagonism, softens the boundaries of a collective identity, keeping it relatively open-ended; and in the rhetoric of testimony, where loss figures subjectivity through recounting the experience of trauma. In fact, however, these two types of rhetoric imply different versions of the same ethico-political concern, although each brings its own risks. They both instantiate a reflexive awareness that the limits of being are precisely what motivates and compels us to speak. Rather than fantasise about fully overcoming these limits, a psychopolitical attitude might contribute to a more engaged but less destructive orientation to speech and argument.

The discussion pursued in this book has been primarily theoretical. Doubtless it has been insufficiently attentive to many of the wider concerns of both psychoanalytical theory and rhetorical enquiry. In my defence, I should underline that my aim has been to sketch a broad landscape rather than to register the finer details and nuances in each approach. In this, I hope nonetheless to open an agenda for understanding the way that argument, in its many various forms and strategies, enacts unconscious dispositions to an ontological incompleteness that is both the source and target of human desire. We argue because we are incomplete and we obsess over controversies because our incompleteness both attracts and horrifies us. A psychopolitical approach to public speech invites further exploration of the connections between speaking and corporeality, that is, the urge to give voice to bodily experiences that otherwise overwhelm us and force us to encounter the limits of our being. Although the term 'loss' bears the unavoidably negative connotation of decline, nevertheless it presents that absence of bodily satisfaction as an elusive unity to which we repeatedly, but inventively, return. A psychopolitics of speech, then, might also be regarded as an invitation to keep returning to this generative source of argument in order to discover new and creative ways to dispute our common worlds.

Bibliography

Alexander, J. C. 2012. *Trauma: A social theory.* Cambridge: Polity.

Allington, D. 2018. "'Hitler had a valid argument against some Jews': Repertoires for the denial of antisemitism in Facebook discussion of a survey of attitudes to Jews and Israel", *Discourse, Context, and Media* 24: 129–136.

Alloa, E. 2017. *Resistance of the sensible world: An introduction to Merleau-Ponty*, trans. J. M. Todd. New York: Fordham University Press.

Angerer, M-L. 2015. *Desire after affect*, trans. N. Grindell. London: Rowman & Littlefield International.

Anker, E. R. 2014. *Orgies of feeling: Melodrama and the politics of freedom.* London: Duke University Press.

Arnheim, R. 1997. *Visual thinking.* Berkeley, CA: University of California Press.

Baldwin, Y. G. 2015. *Let's keep talking: Lacanian tales of love, sex, and other catastrophes.* London: Karnak.

Ballacci, G. 2018. *Political theory between philosophy and rhetoric: Politics as transcendence and contingency.* Basingstoke: Palgrave.

Barruchello, G. 2015. 'A classification of classics: Gestalt psychology and the tropes of rhetoric', *New Ideas in Psychology* 36: 10–24.

Bauman, Z. 1993. *Postmodern ethics.* Oxford: Blackwell.

Beard, M. 2017. *Women and power: A manifesto.* London: Profile.

Becker, B. W. and Manoussakis, J. P. 2018. 'Introduction. Real flesh, imaginary bodies – phenomenology and Lacan on embodiment', in *Unconscious incarnations: Psychoanalytic and philosophical perspectives on the body*, eds. B. W. Becker, J. P. Manoussakis, and D. M. Goodman. London: Routledge, pp. 1–20.

Bender, J. and Wellbery, D. E. 1990. 'Rhetoricality: on the Modernist Return of Rhetoric' in *The ends of rhetoric: History, theory, practice*, ed. J. Bender and D. E. Wellbery. Stanford CA: Stanford University Press, pp. 3–39.

Bernard-Donals, M. 2000. 'Ethos, fitness, and Holocaust "testimony": The rhetoric of fragments', *JAC* 20/3: 565–582.

Bernard-Donals, M. and Glejzer, R. 2001. *Between witness and testimony: The Holocaust and the limits of representation*. Albany: State University of New York.

Bitzer, L. F. 1968. 'The Rhetorical situation', *Philosophy & Rhetoric* 1/1: 1–14.

Boothby, R. 1991. *Death and desire: Psychoanalytic theory in Lacan's return to Freud*. London: Routledge.

Boothby, R. 2001. *Freud as philosopher: Metapsychology after Lacan*. London: Routledge.

Boromisza-Habashi, D. 2013. *Speaking hatefully: Culture, communication, and political action in Hungary*. University Park, PA: Pennsylvania State University Press.

Bowie, M. 1991. *Lacan*. London: Harvard University Press.

Brunner, J. 2001. *Freud and the politics of psychoanalysis*. London: Transaction.

Burton, M. I. 2016. *The Truth and Reconciliation Commission*. Athens: Ohio University Press.

Butler, J. 2010. *Frames of war: When is life grievable?* London: Verso.

Caruth, C. 2016. *Unclaimed experience: Trauma, narrative, and history*, 20th anniversary edition. Baltimore: Johns Hopkins University Press.

Cento Bull, A. and Hansen, H. L. 2016. 'On agonistic memory', *Memory Studies* 9/4: 390–404.

Chambre, A. 2016 (May 2). 'Labour suspends councillor over anti-Semitic social media posts', *PoliticsHome*. Retrieved from https://www.politicshome.com/news/uk/social-affairs/discrimination/news/74510/labour-suspends-councillor-over-anti-semitic-social

Churchill, W. 2007. 'We shall fight on the beaches', speech of 4 June 1940 to the House of Commons in *Great British speeches*, ed. S. Heffer. London: Quercus, pp. 166–171.

Cialdini, R. B. 2007. *Influence: The psychology of persuasion*. New York: HarperCollins.

Conley, T. 2010. *Toward a rhetoric of insult*. London: University of Chicago Press.

Connolly, J. 2007. *The State of speech: Rhetoric and political thought in ancient Rome*. Princeton: Princeton University Press.

Connolly, W. E. 2017. *Aspirational fascism: The struggle for multifaceted democracy under Trumpism*. Minneapolis: University of Minnesota Press.

Coole, D. 2007a. *Merleau-Ponty and modern politics after anti-humanism*. London: Rowman & Littlefield.

Coole, D. 2007b. 'Experiencing discourse: Corporeal communications and the embodiment of power', *British Journal of Politics and International Relations* 9/3: 413–433.

Davies, L., and Lukes, S. 2016 (May 27). 'Unravelling the charge of Labour Party anti-Semitism'. *The Morning Star*. Retrieved from https://www.morningstaronline.co.uk/a-8995-Unravelling-the-Charge-of-Labour-Party-Anti-Semitism#.WOya-nA_5DE

Davies, W. 2018. *Nervous states: How feeling took over the world*. London: Jonathan Cape.

Dillon, M. C. 1997. *Merleau-Ponty's ontology*, 2nd edition. Evanston, Il: Northwestern University Press.

Douglass, F. 2016. 'What to the Slave is the Fourth of July' (1852) in *The portable Frederick Douglass*, eds J. Stauffer and H. L. Gates. London: Penguin, pp. 195–222.

Doxtader, E. 2001. 'Making rhetorical history in a time of transition: The occasion, constitution, and representation of South African reconciliation', *Rhetoric and Public Affairs* 4/2: 223–260.

Eagleton, T. 2018. *Radical sacrifice*. Yale: Yale University Press.

Elgot, J. 2017. (March 30). 'Ken Livingstone "brought Labour into disrepute" with Hitler Zionism remarks', *The Guardian*. Retrieved from https://www.theguardian.com/politics/2017/mar/30/ken-livingstone-labour-party-disrepute-hitler-zionism-former-london-mayor

Esposito, R. 2008. *Bíos: Biopolitics and philosophy*, Trans. T. Campbell. London: University of Minnesota Press.

Esposito, R. 2015. *Persons and things: From the body's point of view*. Cambridge: Polity.

Fine, R. 2009. 'Fighting with phantoms: A contribution to the debate on antisemitism in Europe', *Patterns of Prejudice* 43/5: 459–479.

Fink, B. 1999. *A clinical introduction to Lacanian psychoanalysis*. Cambridge, Mass: Harvard University Press.

Fish, S. 1994. *There's no such thing as free speech ... and it's a good thing too*. Oxford: Oxford University Press.

Fish, S. 1999. *The trouble with principle*. London: Harvard University Press.

Fish, S. 2016. *Winning arguments: What works and doesn't work in politics, the bedroom, the courtroom, and the classroom*. Harper: New York.

Foucault, M. 2008. *The birth of biopolitics: Lectures at the Collège de France 1978–1979*, trans. G. Burchell. Basingstoke: Palgrave.

Freud, S. 1953–74. *The standard edition of the complete psychological works of Sigmund Freud*, 24 volumes, ed. J. Strachey. London: Vintage. Cited in the text as 'SE' followed by volume and page number(s).

Frosh, S. 1989. *Psychoanalysis and psychology: Minding the gap*. Basingstoke: Macmillan.

Frosh, S. 2005. *Hate and the "Jewish Science": Anti-Semitism, Nazism and psychoanalysis*. Basingstoke: Palgrave Macmillan.

Frosh, S. 2010. *Psychoanalysis outside the clinic*. Basingstoke: Palgrave Macmillan.

Gaffney, J. 2017. *Leadership and the Labour Party: Narrative and performance*. Basingstoke: Palgrave Macmillan.

Garsten, B. 2006. *Saving persuasion: A defense of rhetoric and judgement*. London: Harvard University Press.

Geroulanos, S. And Meyers, T. 2018. *The human body in the age of catastrophe: Brittleness, integration, science and the Great War*. Chicago, IL: The University of Chicago Press.

Gillard, J. 2012 (10, October). Transcript of Julia Gillard's speech. *The Sydney Morning Herald*. Retrieved from https://www.smh.com.au/politics/federal/transcript-of-julia-gillards-speech-20121010-27c36.html

Glynos, J. 2001. 'The grip of ideology: a Lacanian approach to the theory of ideology', *Journal of political ideologies* 6/2: 191–214.

Grosz, E. 1994. *Volatile bodies: Towards a corporeal feminism*. Bloomington: Indiana University Press.

Habermas, J. 1996a. *Between facts and norms: Contributions to a discourse theory of law and democracy*. Cambridge: Polity.

Habermas, J. 1996b. *The Habermas reader*, ed. W. Outhwaite. Cambridge: Polity.

Harrison, B. 2006. *The resurgence of anti-semitism: Jews, Israel, and liberal opinion*. Plymouth: Rowman & Littlefield.

Hawhee, D. 2004. *Bodily arts: Rhetoric and athletics in ancient Greece*. Austin, TX: University of Texas Press.

Hay, C. 2007. *Why we hate politics*. Cambridge: Polity.

Heinze, E. 2013. 'Review essay: Hate speech and the normative foundations of regulation', *International journal of law in context* 9/4: 590–617.

Herbst, S. 2010. *Rude democracy: Civility and incivility in American Politics*. Philadelphia, PA: Temple University Press.

Hirsh, D. 2016. *Boycott, divestment and sanctions (BDS) and antisemitism* (Pamphlet No. 1), Academic Engagement Network. Retrieved from http://academicengagement.org/wp-content/uploads/2017/03/David-Hirsh-pamphlet.pdf

Hirsh, D. 2018. *Contemporary left antisemitism*. London: Routledge.

Husserl, E. 2012. *Ideas: General introduction to pure phenomenology*, trans. W. R. Boyce Gibson. London: Routledge.

Jamieson, K. H. 1973. 'Generic constraints and the rhetorical situation', *Philosophy & Rhetoric* 6/3: 162–170.

Kearney, R. 2018. 'The hermeneutics of wounds', in *Unconscious incarnations: Psychoanalytic and philosophical perspectives on the body*, eds. B. W. Becker, J. P. Manoussakis, and D. M. Goodman. London: Routledge, pp. 21–42.

Kennedy, J. F. 1999. 'The torch has been passed to a new generation of Americations' (1961) Inaugural Address in *The Penguin book of twentieth-century speeches*, 2nd edition, ed. B. MacArthur. London: Penguin, pp. 297–301.

Kennedy, R. F. 1968 (April 5). 'The mindless menace of violence', Remarks to the Cleveland City Club. Retrieved from https://www.jfklibrary.org/Research/Research-Aids/Ready-Reference/RFK-Speeches/Remarks-of-Senator-Robert-F-Kennedy-to-the-Cleveland-City-Club-Cleveland-Ohio-April-5-1968.aspx

King, M. L. 1999. 'I have a dream' (1963) speech in *The Penguin book of twentieth-century speeches*, 2nd edition, ed. B. MacArthur. London: Penguin, pp. 327–332.

Kingsbury, P. 2007. 'The extimacy of space', *Social & Cultural Geography* 8/2: 235–258.

Klein, M. 1997. *Envy and gratitude and other works 1946–1963*. London: Vintage.

Klein, M., and Riviere, J. 1964. *Love, hate and reparation*. London: Norton & Co.

Klug, A., Rees, E., and Schneider, J. 2016. 'Momentum: A new kind of politics'. *Renewal* 24/2: 36–44.

Konings, M. 2015. *The emotional logic of capitalism: What progressives have missed*. Stanford, CA: Stanford University Press.

Korostelina, K. 2014. *Political insults: How offenses escalate conflict*. Oxford: Oxford University Press.

Lacan, J. 1977. *The four fundamental concepts of psychoanalysis*, trans. A. Sheridan, ed. J-A. Miller. London: Karnac.

Lacan, J. 1988. *The seminar of Jacques Lacan: Book II The ego in Freud's theory and in the technique of psychoanalysis, 1954–1955*, trans. S. Tomaselli, ed. J-A. Miller. London: Norton.

Lacan, J. 1992. *The ethics of psychoanalysis 1959–1960. The seminar of Jacques Lacan, Book VII*, trans. D. Porter. London: Routledge.

Lacan, J. 1998. *The seminar of Jacques Lacan: Book XX On feminine sexuality, the limits of love and knowledge, 1972–1973*, trans. B. Fink, ed. J-A. Miller. London: Norton.

Lacan, J. 2006. *Écrits*, trans. B. Fink. London: Norton.

Lacan, J. 2007. *The other side of psychoanalysis. The Seminar of Jacques Lacan, Book XVII*, trans. R. Grigg. London: Norton.

Lacan, J. 2008. *My teaching*, trans. D. Macey. London: Verso.

Lacan, J. 2013. *On the Names-of-the-Father*, trans. B. Fink. Cambridge: Polity.

Laclau, E. and Mouffe, C. 1985. *Hegemony and socialist strategy: Towards a radical democratic politics*. London: Verso.

Laclau, E. 1996. *Emancipation(s)*. London: Verso.

Lakoff, G. 2002. *Moral politics: How liberals and conservatives think*, 2nd edition. London: University of Chicago Press.

Lakoff, G. and Johnson, M. 1980. *Metaphors we live by*. London: University of Chicago Press.

Lakoff, G. and Johnson, M. 1999. *Philosophy in the flesh: The embodied mind and its challenge to western thought*. New York: Basic Books.

Landes, D. A. 2013. *Merleau-Ponty and the paradoxes of expression*. London: Bloomsbury.

Lang, H. 1986. *Die Sprache und das Unbewusste. Jacques Lacans Grundlegung der Psychoanalyse*. Frankfurt am Main: Suhrkamp.

Lear, J. 1998. *Love and its place in nature: A philosophical interpretation of Freudian psychoanalysis*. London: Yale.

Leebaw, B. 2011. *Judging state-sponsored violence, imagining political change*. Cambridge: Cambridge University Press.

Lefort, C. 1988. *Democracy and political theory*, trans. D. Macey. Cambridge: Polity.

Lowe, K. 2017. *The fear and the freedom: How the Second World War changed us*. London: Penguin.

Lundberg, C. 2012. *Lacan in public: Psychoanalysis and the science of rhetoric*. Tuscaloosa: University of Alabama Press.

MacKendrick, K. 2004. *Word made skin: Figuring language at the surface of flesh*. New York: Fordham University Press.

Marchart, O. 2007. *Post-foundational political thought: Political difference in Nancy, Lefort, Badiou and Laclau*. Edinburgh: Edinburgh University press.

Marcus, G. E. 2002. *The sentimental citizen: Emotion in democratic politics*. Pennsylvania: Pennsylvania University Press.

Martin, J. 2014. *Politics and rhetoric: A critical introduction*. London: Routledge.

Martin, J. 2015. 'Situating speech: A rhetorical approach to political strategy', *Political Studies* 63/1: 25–42.

Martin, J. 2016. 'Capturing desire: Rhetorical strategies and the affectivity of discourse', *British Journal of Politics and International Relations* 18/1: 143–60.

Martin, P. 2016 (July 20). 'Labour Party members clash over dealing with "vile abuse"'. *BBC News*. Retrieved from http://www.bbc.co.uk/news/uk-wales-politics-36850783

Marzano, M. 2007. *La philosophie du corps*. Paris: Presse Universitaires du France.

Mazzocchi, P. 2013. 'Fleshing out the political: Merleau-Ponty, Lefort and the problem of alterity', *Critical Horizons* 14/1: 22–43.

McAfee, N. 2008. *Democracy and the political unconscious*. New York: Columbia University Press.

McGowan, T. 2007. *The real gaze: Film theory after Lacan*. Albany, NY: State University of New York.

McGowan, T. 2013. *Enjoying what we don't have: The political project of psychoanalysis*. London: University of Nebraska Press.

Mendelson, M. 1998. 'The rhetoric of embodiment', *Rhetoric Society Quarterly* 28/4: 29–50.

Mensch, J. R. 2009. *Embodiments: From the body to the body politic*. Evanston, IL: Northwestern University Press.

Merleau-Ponty, M. 1968. *The visible and the invisible*, trans. Alphonso Lingis. Evanston: Northwestern University Press.

Merleau-Ponty, M. 1973. *The prose of the world*, trans. John O'Neill. Evanston: Northwestern University Press.

Merleau-Ponty, M. 2012. *Phenomenology of perception*, trans. D.A. Landes. London: Routledge.

Millar, A. 2006. *Socio-ideological fantasy and the Northern Ireland conflict: the other side*. Manchester: Manchester University Press.

Miller, J-A. 2008. 'Extimacy', *Symptom* 9. Retrieved from http://www.lacan.com/symptom/extimity.html

Minsky, R. 1998. *Psychoanalysis and culture: Contemporary states of mind*. Cambridge: Polity.

Mouffe, C. 2000. *The democratic paradox*. London: Verso.

Murphy, A. R. 2009. *Prodigal nation: Moral decline and divine punishment from New England to 9/11*. New York: Oxford University Press.

Musolff, A. 2004. *Metaphor and political discourse: Analogical reasoning in debates about Europe*. Basingstoke: Palgrave.

Nasio, J-D. 2001. *Cinq leçons sur la théorie de Jacques Lacan*. Paris: Payot & Rivages.

Nasio, J-D. 2013. *Mon corps et ses images*. Paris: Payot & Rivages.

Newman, S. 2019. *Political theology: A critical introduction*. Cambridge: Polity.

Obama, B. 2009. Inaugural Address (January 20). Retrieved from https://obamawhitehouse.archives.gov/blog/2009/01/21/president-barack-obamas-inaugural-address.

Palonen, K. 2019. *Parliamentary thinking: Procedure, rhetoric and time*. Basingstoke: Palgrave.

Parker, I. 2015. *Psychology after psychoanalysis: Psychosocial studies and beyond*. London: Routledge.

Perelman, Ch. 1982. *The realm of rhetoric*. Notre Dame: University of Notre Dame Press.

Phillips, A. 2014. *Becoming Freud: The making of a psychoanalyst*. London: Yale University Press.

Poynton, C. and Lee, A. 2011. 'Affect-ing discourse: towards an embodied discourse analytics', *Social Semiotics* 21/5: 633–644.

Recalcati, M. 2007. *Elogio dell'inconscio: Dodici argomenti in difesa della psicoanalisi*. Milan: Mondadori.

Recalcati, M. 2012a. *Ritratti del desiderio*. Milan: Raffaello Cortina Editore.

Recalcati, M. 2012b. *Jacques Lacan: Desiderio, godimento e soggettivazione*. Milan: Raffaello Cortina.

Recalcati, M. 2012c. 'Hate as a passion of being', *Qui Parle* 20/2: 151–182.

Recalcati, M. 2014. *La forza del desiderio*. Magnano: Edizioni Qiqajon.

Recalcati, M. 2016. 'Il rovesciamento della visione: tra Merleau-Ponty e Lacan', in *Un cammino nella psicoanalisi. Dalla clinica del vuoto al padre della testimonianza (inediti a scritti rari 2003–2013)*, ed. M. G. Fumel. Milan: Mimesis, pp. 155–171.

Recalcati, M. 2017. *Contro il sacrificio: Al di là del fantasma sacrificiale*. Milan: Raffaello Cortina.

Rich, D. 2016. *The left's Jewish problem: Jeremy Corbyn, Israel and anti-Semitism*. London: Biteback.

Richards, B. 2007. *Emotional governance: Politics, media and terror*. Basingstoke: Palgrave.

Roberts-Miller, P. 2017. *Demagoguery and democracy*. New York: The Experiment.

Rothenberg, M. A. 2010. *The excessive subject: A new theory of social change*. Cambridge: Polity.

Ruti, M. 2012. *The singularity of being. Lacan and the immortal within*. New York: Fordham University Press.

Ruti, M. 2014. *The call of character: Living a life worth living*. New York: Columbia University Press.

Saint-Amand, P. 1996. *The laws of hostility: Politics, violence, and the Enlightenment*, trans. J. Curtiss Gage. London: University of Minnesota Press.

Santner, E. L. 2011. *The royal remains: The people's two bodies and the endgames of sovereignty*. London: University of Chicago Press.

Sartre, J-P. 2013. 'A fundamental idea of Husserl's phenomenology: Intentionality', *We have only this life to live: The selected essays of Jean-Paul Sartre 1939–1975*, eds. R. Aronson and A. Van den Hoven. New York: New York Review of Books, pp. 3–6.

Saxonhouse, A. 1992. *Fear of diversity: The birth of political science in ancient Greek thought.* London: University of Chicago Press.
Sheer, M. and Haberman, M. D. 2017. 'Trump defends initial remarks on Charlottesville; again blames "both sides"', *The New York Times* (August 15). Retrieved from https://www.nytimes.com/2017/08/15/us/politics/trump-press-conference-charlottesville.html
Sinnott-Armstrong, W. 2018. *Think again: How to reason and argue.* London: Pelican.
Solomon, T. 2015. *The politics of subjectivity in American foreign policy discourses.* Ann Arbor: University of Michigan Press.
Stavrakakis, Y. 1999. *Lacan and the political.* London: Routledge.
Thaler, R. H. and Sunstein, C. R. 2009. *Nudge: improving decisions about health, wealth and happiness.* London: Penguin.
Thompson, P. 2016 (August 24). 'Corbynism isn't a social movement and Labour shouldn't be one', *Renewal* [Blog post]. Retrieved from www.renewal.org.uk/blog/corbynism-isnt-a-social-movement-and-labour-shouldnt-be-one
Trigg, D. 2014. *The thing: A phenomenology of horror.* Winchester: Zero Books.
Trigg, D. 2017. *Topophobia: A phenomenology of anxiety.* London: Bloomsbury.
Trump, D. J. 2017. Inaugural Address. Retrieved from: https://www.whitehouse.gov/briefings-statements/the-inaugural-address/
Tucker, R. E. 2001. 'Figure, ground and presence: A phenomenology of meaning in rhetoric', *Quarterly Journal of Speech* 87/4: 396–414.
Turkle, S. 2015. *Relcaiming conversation: The power of talk in a digital age.* New York: Penguin.
Turnbull, N. 2017. 'Political rhetoric and its relationship to context: a new theory of the rhetorical situation, the rhetorical and the political', *Critical Discourse Studies* 14/2: 115–31.
Vanheule, S. 2014. *The subject of psychosis: A Lacanian perspective.* Basingstoke: Palgrave Macmillan.
Vatz, R. E. 1973. 'The myth of the rhetorical situation', *Philosophy & Rhetoric* 6/3: 154–61.

Waldron, J. 2012. *The harm in hate speech*. London: Harvard University Press.

Waltman, M., and Haas, J. 2011. *The communication of hate*. Oxford: Peter Lang.

Webb, S. H. 1993. *Blessed excess: Religion and the hyperbolic imagination*. Albany: State University of New York.

Wetherell, M. 2012. *Affect and emotion: A new social science understanding*. London: Sage.

Woods, J. 2004. *The death of argument: Fallacies in agent based reasoning*. London: Springer Science.

Wright, E. 1999. *Speaking desires can be dangerous: The poetics of the unconscious*. Cambridge: Polity.

Yadron, D. 2016. 'Zuckerberg on telepathy: you'll capture a thought and share it with the world', *The Guardian* (Wednesday, 15 June). Retrieved from https://www.theguardian.com/technology/2016/jun/14/zuckerberg-telepathy-facebook-live-video-seinfeld

Yanay, N. 2013. *The ideology of hatred: The psychic power of discourse*. New York: Fordham University Press.

Zaretsky, E. 2015. *Political Freud: A history*. New York: Columbia University Press.

Žižek, S. 1989. *The sublime object of ideology*. London: Verso.

Žižek, S. 1994. *The metastases of enjoyment: On women and causality*. London: Verso.